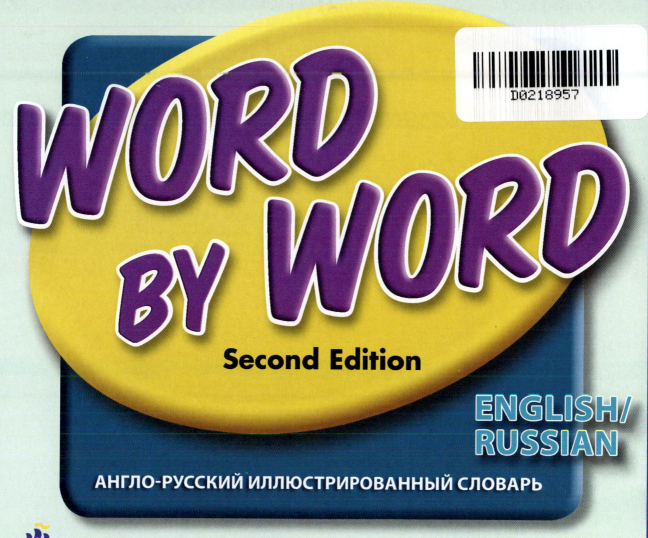

WORD BY WORD

Second Edition

ENGLISH/RUSSIAN

АНГЛО-РУССКИЙ ИЛЛЮСТРИРОВАННЫЙ СЛОВАРЬ

Steven J. Molinsky • Bill Bliss

Maria Brezinsky, John T. Brezinsky–Translators

Illustrated by
Richard E. Hill

Word by Word Picture Dictionary,
English/Russian second edition

Pearson Education, 10 Bank Street, White Plains, NY 10606

Editorial director: Pam Fishman
Vice president, director of design and
production: Rhea Banker
Director of electronic production: Aliza Greenblatt
Director of manufacturing: Patrice Fraccio
Senior manufacturing manager: Edith Pullman
Marketing manager: Oliva Fernandez
Associate development editor: Mary Perrotta Rich

Assistant editor: Katherine Keyes
Senior digital layout specialist: Wendy Wolf
Text design: Wendy Wolf
Cover design: Tracey Munz Cataldo
Realia creation: Warren Fischbach, Paula Williams
Illustrations: Richard E. Hill
Contributing artists: Steven Young, Charles Cawley,
Willard Gage, Marlon Violette
Reviewer: Lyudmila Dragushanskaya, ASA Institute
Project management by TransPac Education Services,
Victoria, BC, Canada with assistance from Robert Zacharias

ISBN-10 0-13-191632-7   ISBN-13 9780131916326

Longman on the Web
Longman.com offers online resources for teachers and
students. Access our Companion Websites, our online
catalog, and our local offices around the world.

Visit us at www.pearsonlongman.com.

Printed in the United States of America
1 2 3 4 5 6 7 8 9 10 – QWD – 12 11 10 09 08

CONTENTS
СОДЕРЖАНИЕ

Unit / Theme	Communication Skills	Writing & Discussion
1 Personal Information and Family	• Asking for & giving personal information • Identifying information on a form • Spelling name aloud • Identifying family members • Introducing others	• Telling about yourself • Telling about family members • Drawing a family tree
2 Common Everyday Activities and Language	• Identifying classroom objects & locations • Identifying classroom actions • Giving & following simple classroom commands • Identifying everyday & leisure activities • Inquiring by phone about a person's activities • Asking about a person's plan for future activities • Social communication: Greeting people, Leave taking, Introducing yourself & others, Getting someone's attention, Expressing gratitude, Saying you don't understand, Calling someone on the telephone • Describing the weather • Interpreting temperatures on a thermometer (Fahrenheit & Centigrade) • Describing the weather forecast for tomorrow	• Describing a classroom • Making a list of daily activities • Describing daily routine • Making a list of planned activities • Describing favorite leisure activities • Describing the weather
3 Numbers/ Time/ Money/ Calendar	• Using cardinal & ordinal numbers • Giving information about age, number of family members, residence • Telling time • Indicating time of events • Asking for information about arrival & departure times • Identifying coins & currency – names & values • Making & asking for change • Identifying days of the week • Identifying months of the year • Asking about the year, month, day, date • Asking about the date of a birthday, anniversary, appointment • Giving date of birth	• Describing numbers of students in a class • Identifying a country's population • Describing daily schedule with times • Telling about time management • Telling about the use of time in different cultures or countries • Describing the cost of purchases • Describing coins & currency of other countries • Describing weekday & weekend activities • Telling about favorite day of the week & month of the year
4 Home	• Identifying types of housing & communities • Requesting a taxi • Calling 911 for an ambulance • Identifying rooms of a home • Identifying furniture • Complimenting • Asking for information in a store • Locating items in a store • Asking about items on sale • Asking the location of items at home • Telling about past weekend activities • Identifying locations in an apartment building • Identifying ways to look for housing: classified ads, listings, vacancy signs • Renting an apartment • Describing household problems • Securing home repair services • Making a suggestion • Identifying household cleaning items, home supplies, & tools • Asking to borrow an item • Describing current home activities & plans for future activities	• Describing types of housing where people live • Describing rooms & furniture in a residence • Telling about baby products & early child-rearing practices in different countries • Telling about personal experiences with repairing things • Describing an apartment building • Describing household cleaning chores
5 Community	• Identifying places in the community • Exchanging greetings • Asking & giving the location of places in the community • Identifying government buildings, services, & other places in a city/town center • Identifying modes of transportation in a city/town center	• Describing places in a neighborhood • Making a list of places, people, & actions observed at an intersection

Unit / Theme	Communication Skills	Writing & Discussion
6 Describing	• Describing people by age • Describing people by physical characteristics • Describing a suspect or missing person to a police officer • Describing people & things using adjectives • Describing physical states & emotions • Expressing concern about another person's physical state or emotion	• Describing physical characteristics of yourself & family members • Describing physical characteristics of a favorite actor or actress or other famous person • Describing things at home & in the community • Telling about personal experiences with different emotions
7 Food	• Identifying food items (fruits, vegetables, meat, poultry, seafood, dairy products, juices, beverages, deli, frozen foods, snack foods, groceries) • Identifying non-food items purchased in a supermarket (e.g., household supplies, baby products, pet food) • Determining food needs to make a shopping list • Asking the location of items in a supermarket • Identifying supermarket sections • Requesting items at a service counter in a supermarket • Identifying supermarket checkout area personnel & items • Identifying food containers & quantities • Identifying units of measure • Asking for & giving recipe instructions • Complimenting someone on a recipe • Offering to help with food preparation • Identifying food preparation actions • Identifying kitchen utensils & cookware • Asking to borrow an item • Comprehending product advertising • Ordering fast food items, coffee shop items, & sandwiches • Indicating a shortage of supplies to a co-worker or supervisor • Taking customers' orders at a food service counter • Identifying restaurant objects, personnel, & actions • Making & following requests at work • Identifying & correctly positioning silverware & plates in a table setting • Inquiring in person about restaurant job openings • Ordering from a restaurant menu • Taking customers' orders as a waiter or waitress in a restaurant	• Describing favorite & least favorite foods • Describing foods in different countries • Making a shopping list • Describing places to shop for food • Telling about differences between supermarkets & food stores in different countries • Making a list of items in kitchen cabinets & the refrigerator • Describing recycling practices • Describing a favorite recipe using units of measure • Telling about use of kitchen utensils & cookware • Telling about experience with different types of restaurants • Describing restaurants and menus in different countries • Describing favorite foods ordered in restaurants
8 Colors and Clothing	• Identifying colors • Complimenting someone on clothing • Identifying clothing items, including outerwear, sleepwear, underwear, exercise clothing, footwear, jewelry, & accessories • Talking about appropriate clothing for different weather conditions • Expressing clothing needs to a store salesperson • Locating clothing items • Inquiring about ownership of found clothing items • Indicating loss of a clothing item • Asking about sale prices in a clothing store • Reporting theft of a clothing item to the police • Stating preferences during clothing shopping • Expressing problems with clothing & the need for alterations • Identifying laundry objects & activities • Locating laundry products in a store	• Describing the flags of different countries • Telling about emotions associated with different colors • Telling about clothing & colors you like to wear • Describing clothing worn at different occasions (e.g., going to schools, parties, weddings) • Telling about clothing worn in different weather conditions • Telling about clothing worn during exercise activities • Telling about footwear worn during different activities • Describing the color, material, size, & pattern of favorite clothing items • Comparing clothing fashions now & a long time ago • Telling about who does laundry at home

Unit / Theme	Communication Skills	Writing & Discussion
9 **Shopping**	• Identifying departments & services in a department store • Asking the location of items in a department store • Asking to buy, return, exchange, try on, & pay for department store items • Asking about regular & sales prices, discounts, & sales tax • Interpreting a sales receipt • Offering assistance to customers as a salesperson • Expressing needs to a salesperson in a store • Identifying electronics products, including video & audio equipment, telephones, cameras, & computers • Identifying components of a computer & common computer software • Complimenting someone about an item & inquiring where it was purchased • Asking a salesperson for advice about different brands of a product • Identifying common toys & other items in a toy store • Asking for advice about an appropriate gift for a child	• Describing a department store • Telling about stores that have sales • Telling about an item purchased on sale • Comparing different types & brands of video & audio equipment • Describing telephones & cameras • Describing personal use of a computer • Sharing opinions about how computers have changed the world • Telling about popular toys in different countries • Telling about favorite childhood toys
10 **Community Services**	• Requesting bank services & transactions (e.g., deposit, withdrawal, cashing a check, obtaining traveler's checks, opening an account, applying for a loan, exchanging currency) • Identifying bank personnel • Identifying bank forms • Asking about acceptable forms of payment (cash, check, credit card, money order, traveler's check) • Identifying household bills (rent, utilities, etc.) • Identifying family finance documents & actions • Following instructions to use an ATM machine • Requesting post office services & transactions • Identifying types of mail & mail services • Identifying different ways to buy stamps • Requesting non-mail services available at the post office (money order, selective service registration, passport application) • Identifying & locating library sections, services, & personnel • Asking how to find a book in the library • Identifying community institutions, services, and personnel (police, fire, city government, public works, recreation, sanitation, religious institutions) • Identifying types of emergency vehicles • Reporting a crime • Identifying community mishaps (gas leak, water main break, etc.) • Expressing concern about community problems	• Describing use of bank services • Telling about household bills & amounts paid • Telling about the person responsible for household finances • Describing use of ATM machines • Describing use of postal services • Comparing postal systems in different countries • Telling about experience using a library • Telling about the location of community institutions • Describing experiences using community institutions • Telling about crime in the community • Describing experience with a crime or emergency
11 **Health**	• Identifying parts of the body & key internal organs • Describing ailments, symptoms, & injuries • Asking about the health of another person • Identifying items in a first-aid kit • Describing medical emergencies • Identifying emergency medical procedures (CPR, rescue breathing, Heimlich maneuver) • Calling 911 to report a medical emergency • Identifying major illnesses • Talking with a friend or co-worker about illness in one's family • Following instructions during a medical examination • Identifying medical personnel, equipment, & supplies in medical & dental offices • Understanding medical & dental personnel's description of procedures during treatment • Understanding a doctor's medical advice and instructions • Identifying over-the-counter medications • Understanding dosage instructions on medicine labels • Identifying medical specialists • Indicating the date & time of a medical appointment • Identifying hospital departments & personnel • Identifying equipment in a hospital room • Identifying actions & items related to personal hygiene • Locating personal care products in a store • Identifying actions & items related to baby care	• Describing self • Telling about a personal experience with an illness or injury • Describing remedies or treatments for common problems (cold, stomachache, insect bite, hiccups) • Describing experience with a medical emergency • Describing a medical examination • Describing experience with a medical or dental procedure • Telling about medical advice received • Telling about over-the-counter medications used • Comparing use of medications in different countries • Describing experience with a medical specialist • Describing a hospital stay • Making a list of personal care items needed for a trip • Comparing baby products in different countries

Unit / Theme	Communication Skills	Writing & Discussion

12 School, Subjects, and Activities	• Identifying types of educational institutions
	• Giving information about previous education during a job interview
	• Identifying school locations & personnel
	• Identifying school subjects
	• Identifying extracurricular activities
	• Sharing after-school plans
	• MATH:
	  • Asking & answering basic questions during a math class
	  • Using fractions to indicate sale prices
	  • Using percents to indicate test scores & probability in weather forecasts
	  • Identifying high school math subjects
	  • Using measurement terms to indicate height, width, depth, length, distance
	  • Interpreting metric measurements
	  • Identifying types of lines, geometric shapes, & solid figures
	• ENGLISH LANGUAGE ARTS:
	  • Identifying types of sentences
	  • Identifying parts of speech
	  • Identifying punctuation marks
	  • Providing feedback during peer-editing
	  • Identifying steps of the writing process
	  • Identifying types of literature
	  • Identifying forms of writing
	• GEOGRAPHY:
	  • Identifying geographical features & bodies of water
	  • Identifying natural environments (desert, jungle, rainforest, etc.)
	• SCIENCE:
	  • Identifying science classroom/laboratory equipment
	  • Asking about equipment needed to do a science procedure
	  • Identifying steps of the scientific method
	  • Identifying key terms to describe the universe, solar system, & space exploration
		• Telling about different types of schools in the community
		• Telling about schools attended, where, when, & subjects studied
		• Describing a school
		• Comparing schools in different countries
		• Telling about favorite school subject
		• Telling about extracurricular activities
		• Comparing extracurricular activities in different countries
		• Describing math education
		• Telling about something bought on sale
		• Researching & sharing information about population statistics using percents
		• Describing favorite books & authors
		• Describing newspapers & magazines read
		• Telling about use of different types of written communication
		• Describing the geography of your country
		• Describing geographical features experienced
		• Describing experience with scientific equipment
		• Describing science education
		• Brainstorming a science experiment & describing each step of the scientific method
		• Drawing & naming a constellation
		• Expressing an opinion about the importance of space exploration

13 Work	• Identifying occupations • Stating work experience (including length of time in an occupation) during a job interview • Talking about occupation during social conversation • Expressing job aspirations • Identifying job skills & work activities • Indicating job skills during an interview (including length of time) • Identifying types of job advertisements (help wanted signs, job notices, classified ads) • Interpreting abbreviations in job advertisements • Identifying each step in a job-search process • Identifying workplace locations, furniture, equipment, & personnel • Identifying common office tasks • Asking the location of a co-worker • Engaging in small-talk with co-workers • Identifying common office supplies • Making requests at work • Repeating to confirm understanding of a request or instruction • Identifying factory locations, equipment, & personnel • Asking the location of workplace departments & personnel to orient oneself as a new employee • Asking about the location & activities of a co-worker • Identifying construction site machinery, equipment, and building materials • Asking a co-worker for a workplace item • Warning a co-worker of a safety hazard • Asking whether there is a sufficient supply of workplace materials • Identifying job safety equipment • Interpreting warning signs at work • Reminding someone to use safety equipment • Asking the location of emergency equipment at work	• Career exploration: sharing ideas about occupations that are interesting, difficult • Describing occupation & occupations of family members • Describing job skills • Describing a familiar job (skill requirements, qualifications, hours, salary) • Telling about how people found their jobs • Telling about experience with a job search or job interview • Describing a familiar workplace • Telling about office & school supplies used • Describing a nearby factory & working conditions there • Comparing products produced by factories in different countries • Describing building materials used in ones dwelling • Describing a nearby construction site • Telling about experience with safety equipment • Describing the use of safety equipment in the community

Unit / Theme	Communication Skills	Writing & Discussion
14 **Transportation and Travel**	• Identifying modes of local & inter-city public transportation • Expressing intended mode of travel • Asking about a location to obtain transportation (bus stop, bus station, train station, subway station) • Locating ticket counters, information booths, fare card machines, & information signage in transportation stations • Identifying types of vehicles • Indicating to a car salesperson need for a type of vehicle • Describing a car accident • Identifying parts of a car & maintenance items • Indicating a problem with a car • Requesting service or assistance at a service station • Identifying types of highway lanes & markings, road structures (tunnels, bridges, etc.), traffic signage, & local intersection road markings • Reporting the location of an accident • Giving & following driving directions (using prepositions of motion) • Interpreting traffic signs • Warning a driver about an upcoming sign • Interpreting compass directions • Asking for driving directions • Following instructions during a driver's test • Repeating to confirm instructions • Identifying airport locations & personnel (check-in, security, gate, baggage claim, Customs & Immigration) • Asking for location of places & personnel at an airport • Indicating loss of travel documents or other items • Identifying airplane sections, seating areas, emergency equipment, & flight personnel • Identifying steps in the process of airplane travel (actions in the security area, at the gate, boarding, & being seated) • Following instructions of airport security personnel, gate attendants, & flight crew • Identifying sections of a hotel & personnel • Asking for location of places & personnel in a hotel	• Describing mode of travel to different places in the community • Describing local public transportation • Comparing transportation in different countries • Telling about common types of vehicles in different countries • Expressing opinion about favorite type of vehicle & manufacturer • Expressing opinion about most important features to look for when making a car purchase • Describing experience with car repairs • Describing a local highway • Describing a local intersection • Telling about dangerous traffic areas where many accidents occur • Describing your route from home to school • Describing how to get to different places from home and school • Describing local traffic signs • Comparing traffic signs in different countries • Describing a familiar airport • Telling about an experience with Customs & Immigration • Describing an air travel experience • Using imagination: being an airport security officer giving passengers instructions; being a flight attendant giving passengers instructions before take-off • Describing a familiar hotel • Expressing opinion about hotel jobs that are most interesting, most difficult
15 **Recreation and Entertainment**	• Identifying common hobbies, crafts, & games & related materials/equipment • Describing favorite leisure activities • Purchasing craft supplies, equipment, & other products in a store • Asking for & offering a suggestion for a leisure activity • Identifying places to go for outdoor recreation, entertainment, culture, etc. • Describing past weekend activities • Describing activities planned for a future day off or weekend • Identifying features & equipment in a park & playground • Asking the location of a park feature or equipment • Warning a child to be careful on playground equipment • Identifying features of a beach, common beach items, & personnel • Identifying indoor & outdoor recreation activities & sports, & related equipment & supplies • Asking if someone remembered an item when preparing for an activity • Identifying team sports & terms for players, playing fields, & equipment • Commenting on a player's performance during a game • Indicating that you can't find an item • Asking the location of sports equipment in a store • Reminding someone of items needed for a sports activity • Identifying types of winter/water sports, recreation, & equipment • Engaging in small talk about favorite sports & recreation activities • Using the telephone to inquire whether a store sells a product • Making & responding to an invitation • Following a teacher or coach's instructions during sports practice, P.E. class, & an exercise class • Identifying types of entertainment & cultural events, & the performers • Commenting on a performance • Identifying genres of music, plays, movies, & TV programs • Expressing likes about types of entertainment • Identifying musical instruments • Complimenting someone on musical ability	• Describing a favorite hobby, craft, or game • Comparing popular games in different countries, and how to play them • Describing favorite places to go & activities there • Describing a local park & playground • Describing a favorite beach & items used there • Describing an outdoor recreation experience • Describing favorite individual sports & recreation activities • Describing favorite team sports & famous players • Comparing popular sports in different countries • Describing experience with winter or water sports & recreation • Expressing opinions about Winter Olympics sports (most exciting, most dangerous) • Describing exercise habits & routines • Using imagination: being an exercise instructor leading a class • Telling about favorite types of entertainment • Comparing types of entertainment popular in different countries • Telling about favorite performers • Telling about favorite types of music, movies, & TV programs • Describing experience with a musical instrument • Comparing typical musical instruments in different countries

Unit / Theme	Communication Skills	Writing & Discussion
16 Nature	• Identifying places & people on a farm • Identifying farm animals & crops • Identifying animals & pets • Identifying birds & insects • Identifying fish, sea animals, amphibians, & reptiles • Asking about the presence of wildlife in an area • Identifying trees, plants, & flowers • Identifying key parts of a tree and flower • Asking for information about trees & flowers • Warning someone about poisonous vegetation in an area • Identifying sources of energy • Describing the kind of energy used to heat homes & for cooking • Expressing an opinion about good future sources of energy • Identifying behaviors that promote conservation (recycling, conserving energy, conserving water, carpooling) • Expressing concern about environmental problems • Identifying different kinds of natural disasters	• Comparing farms in different countries • Telling about local animals, animals in a zoo, & common local birds & insects • Comparing common pets in different countries • Using imagination: what animal you would like to be, & why • Telling a popular folk tale or children's story about animals, birds, or insects • Describing fish, sea animals, & reptiles in different countries • Identifying endangered species • Expressing opinions about wildlife – most interesting, beautiful, dangerous • Describing local trees & flowers, & favorites • Comparing different cultures' use of flowers at weddings, funerals, holidays, & hospitals • Expressing an opinion about an environmental problem • Telling about how people prepare for natural disasters
17 U.S. Civics	• Producing correct form of identification when requested (driver's license, social security card, student I.D. card, employee I.D. badge, permanent resident card, passport, visa, work permit, birth certificate, proof of residence) • Identifying the three branches of U.S. government (legislative, executive, judicial) & their functions • Identifying senators, representatives, the president, vice-president, cabinet, Supreme Court justices, & the chief justice, & the branches of government in which they work • Identifying the key buildings in each branch of government (Capitol Building, White House, Supreme Court Building) • Identifying the Constitution as "the supreme law of the land" • Identifying the Bill of Rights • Naming freedoms guaranteed by the 1st Amendment • Identifying key amendments to the Constitution • Identifying key events in United States history • Answering history questions about events and the dates they occurred • Identifying key holidays & dates they occur • Identifying legal system & court procedures (arrest, booking, obtaining legal representation, appearing in court, standing trial, acquittal, conviction, sentencing, prison, release) • Identifying people in the criminal justice system • Engaging in small talk about a TV crime show's characters & plot • Identifying rights & responsibilities of U.S. citizens • Identifying steps in applying for citizenship	• Telling about forms of identification & when needed • Describing how people in a community "exercise their 1st Amendment rights" • Brainstorming ideas for a new amendment to the Constitution • Expressing an opinion about the most important event in United States history • Telling about important events in the history of different countries • Describing U.S. holidays you celebrate • Describing holidays celebrated in different countries • Describing the legal system in different countries • Telling about an episode of a TV crime show • Expressing an opinion about the most important rights & responsibilities of people in their communities • Expressing an opinion about the rights of citizens vs. non-citizens

Welcome to the second edition of the WORD BY WORD Picture Dictionary! This text presents more than 4,000 vocabulary words through vibrant illustrations and simple accessible lesson pages that are designed for clarity and ease-of-use with learners at all levels. Our goal is to prepare students for success using English in everyday life, in the community, in school, and at work.

WORD BY WORD organizes the vocabulary into 17 thematic units, providing a careful research-based sequence of lessons that integrates students' development of grammar and vocabulary skills through topics that begin with the immediate world of the student and progress to the world at large. Early lessons on the family, the home, and daily activities lead to lessons on the community, school, workplace, shopping, recreation, and other topics. The text offers extensive coverage of important lifeskill competencies and the vocabulary of school subjects and extracurricular activities, and it is designed to meet the objectives of current national, state, and local standards-based curricula you can find in the Scope & Sequence on the previous pages.

Since each lesson in *Word by Word* is self-contained, it can be used either sequentially or in any desired order. For users' convenience, the lessons are listed in two ways: sequentially in the Table of Contents, and alphabetically in the Thematic Index. These resources, combined with the Glossary in the appendix, allow students and teachers to quickly and easily locate all words and topics in the Picture Dictionary.

The *Word by Word* Picture Dictionary is the centerpiece of the complete *Word by Word* Vocabulary Development Program, which offers a wide selection of print and media support materials for instruction at all levels.

A unique choice of workbooks at Beginning and Intermediate levels offers flexible options to meet students' needs. Vocabulary Workbooks feature motivating vocabulary, grammar, and listening practice, and standards-based Lifeskills Workbooks provide competency-based activities and reading tied to national, state, and local curriculum frameworks. A Literacy Workbook is also available.

The Teacher's Guide and Lesson Planner with CD-ROM includes lesson-planning suggestions, community tasks, Internet weblinks, and reproducible masters to save teachers hours of lesson preparation time. An Activity Handbook with step-by-step teaching strategies for key vocabulary development activities is included in the Teacher's Guide.

The Audio Program includes all words and conversations for interactive practice and —as bonus material—an expanded selection of WordSongs for entertaining musical practice with the vocabulary.

Additional ancillary materials include Color Transparencies, Vocabulary Game Cards, and a Testing Program. Bilingual Editions are also available.

Teaching Strategies

Word by Word presents vocabulary words in context. Model conversations depict situations in which people use the words in meaningful communication. These models become the basis for students to engage in dynamic, interactive practice. In addition, writing and discussion questions in each lesson encourage students to relate the vocabulary and themes to their own lives as they share experiences, thoughts, opinions, and information about themselves, their cultures, and their countries. In this way, students get to know each other "word by word."

In using *Word by Word*, we encourage you to develop approaches and strategies that are compatible with your own teaching style and the needs and abilities of your students. You may find it helpful to incorporate some of the following techniques for presenting and practicing the vocabulary in each lesson.

1. **Preview the Vocabulary:** Activate students' prior knowledge of the vocabulary by brainstorming with students the words in the lesson they already know and writing them on the board, or by having students look at the transparency or the illustration in *Word by Word* and identify the words they are familiar with.

2. **Present the Vocabulary:** Using the transparency or the illustration in the Picture Dictionary, point to the picture of each word, say the word, and have the class repeat it chorally and individually. (You can also play the word list on the Audio Program.) Check students' understanding and pronunciation of the vocabulary.

3. **Vocabulary Practice:** Have students practice the vocabulary as a class, in pairs, or in small groups. Say or write a word, and have students point to the item or tell the number. Or, point to an item or give the number, and have students say the word.

4. **Model Conversation Practice:** Some lessons have model conversations that use the first word in the vocabulary list. Other models are in the form of skeletal dialogs, in which vocabulary words can be inserted. (In many skeletal dialogs, bracketed numbers indicate which words can be used for practicing the conversation. If no bracketed numbers appear, all the words in the lesson can be used.)

The following steps are recommended for Model Conversation Practice:

a. Preview: Have students look at the model illustration and discuss who they think the speakers are and where the conversation takes place.

b. The teacher presents the model or plays the audio one or more times and checks students' understanding of the situation and the vocabulary.

c. Students repeat each line of the conversation chorally and individually.

d. Students practice the model in pairs.

e. A pair of students presents a conversation based on the model, but using a different word from the vocabulary list.

f. In pairs, students practice several conversations based on the model, using different words on the page.

g. Pairs present their conversations to the class.

5. **Additional Conversation Practice:** Many lessons provide two additional skeletal dialogs for further conversation practice with the vocabulary. (These can be found in the yellow-shaded area at the bottom of the page.) Have students practice and present these conversations using any words they wish. Before they practice the additional conversations, you may want to have students listen to the sample additional conversations on the Audio Program.

6. **Spelling Practice:** Have students practice spelling the words as a class, in pairs, or in small groups. Say a word, and have students spell it aloud or write it. Or, using the transparency, point to an item and have students write the word.

7. **Themes for Discussion, Composition, Journals, and Portfolios:** Each lesson of *Word by Word* provides one or more questions for discussion and composition. (These can be found in a blue-shaded area at the bottom of the page.) Have students respond to the questions as a class, in pairs, or in small groups. Or, have students write their responses at home, share their written work with other students, and discuss as a class, in pairs, or in small groups.

Students may enjoy keeping a journal of their written work. If time permits, you may want to write a response in each student's journal, sharing your own opinions and experiences as well as reacting to what the student has written. If you are keeping portfolios of students' work, these compositions serve as excellent examples of students' progress in learning English.

8. **Communication Activities:** The *Word by Word* Teacher's Guide and Lesson Planner with CD-ROM provides a wealth of games, tasks, brainstorming, discussion, movement, drawing, miming, role-playing, and other activities designed to take advantage of students' different learning styles and particular abilities and strengths. For each lesson, choose one or more of these activities to reinforce students' vocabulary learning in a way that is stimulating, creative, and enjoyable.

WORD BY WORD aims to offer students a communicative, meaningful, and lively way of practicing English vocabulary. In conveying to you the substance of our program, we hope that we have also conveyed the spirit: that learning vocabulary can be genuinely interactive . . . relevant to our students' lives . . . responsive to students' differing strengths and learning styles . . . and fun!

Steven J. Molinsky

Bill Bliss

ЛИЧНЫЕ ДАННЫЕ

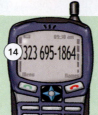

Registration Form

Name _____ Gloria _____ P. _____ Sánchez _____
First   Middle Initial   Last

Address _____ 95 _____ Garden Street _____ 3G _____
Number   Street   Apartment Number
Los Angeles _____ CA _____ 90036 _____
City   State   Zip Code

Telephone _323-524-3278_   Cell Phone _323-695-1864_

E-Mail Address _gloria97@ail.com_   SSN _227-93-6185_   Sex M_   F X

Date of Birth _5/12/88_   Place of Birth _Centerville, Texas_

имя	**1**	name
имя	**2**	first name
инициал отчества	**3**	middle initial
фамилия	**4**	last name / family name / surname
адрес	**5**	address
номер дома	**6**	street number
улица	**7**	street
номер квартиры	**8**	apartment number
город	**9**	city
штат	**10**	state
индекс	**11**	zip code
код города	**12**	area code
номер телефона	**13**	telephone number / phone number
номер мобильного телефона	**14**	cell phone number
адрес электронной почты	**15**	e-mail address
номер социального обеспечения	**16**	social security number
пол	**17**	sex
дата рождения	**18**	date of birth
место рождения	**19**	place of birth

A. What's your **name**?
B. Gloria P. Sánchez.

A. What's your _____?
B. ....
A. Did you say ....?
B. Yes. That's right.

A. What's your last name?
B. ....
A. How do you spell that?
B. ....

Tell about yourself:
   My name is ....
   My address is ....
   My telephone number is ....

Now interview a friend.

муж	**1** husband	дети	**children**	дедушка и бабушка	**grandparents**
жена	**2** wife	дочь	**5** daughter	бабушка	**10** grandmother
		сын	**6** son	дедушка	**11** grandfather
родители	**parents**	ребёнок	**7** baby		
отец	**3** father			**внуки**	**grandchildren**
мать	**4** mother	**братья и сёстры**	**siblings**	внучка	**12** granddaughter
		сестра	**8** sister	внук	**13** grandson
		брат	**9** brother		

A. Who is he?
B. He's my **husband**.
A. What's his name?
B. His name is *Jack*.

A. Who is she?
B. She's my **wife**.
A. What's her name?
B. Her name is *Nancy*.

A. I'd like to introduce my _____.
B. Nice to meet you.
C. Nice to meet you, too.

A. What's your _____'s name?
B. His/Her name is ....

Who are the people in your family?
What are their names?

Tell about photos of family members.

ЧЛЕНЫ СЕМЬИ II

дядя	**1**	uncle
тётя	**2**	aunt
племянница	**3**	niece
племянник	**4**	nephew
двоюродная сестра/брат	**5**	cousin

свекровь	**6**	mother-in-law
свёкор	**7**	father-in-law
зять	**8**	son-in-law
невестка/сноха	**9**	daughter-in-law
шурин/деверь/зять/свояк	**10**	brother-in-law
свояченица/невестка/золовка	**11**	sister-in-law

1. Jack is Alan's ____.
2. Nancy is Alan's ____.
3. Jennifer is Frank and Linda's ____.
4. Timmy is Frank and Linda's ____.
5. Alan is Jennifer and Timmy's ____.

6. Helen is Jack's ____.
7. Walter is Jack's ____.
8. Jack is Helen and Walter's ____.
9. Linda is Helen and Walter's ____.
10. Frank is Jack's ____.
11. Linda is Jack's ____.

A. Who is he/she?
B. He's/She's my _____.
A. What's his/her name?
B. His/Her name is _____.

A. Let me introduce my _____.
B. I'm glad to meet you.
C. Nice meeting you, too.

Tell about your relatives:
What are their names?
Where do they live?

Draw your family tree and tell about it.

4

учитель	**1**	teacher	экран	**9**	screen	белая доска/	**15**	whiteboard/
лаборант	**2**	teacher's aide	меловая доска/	**10**	chalkboard/	доска		board
студент	**3**	student	доска		board	глобус	**16**	globe
парта	**4**	desk	часы	**11**	clock	книжный шкаф/	**17**	bookcase/
стул	**5**	seat/chair	карта	**12**	map	книжная полка		bookshelf
стол	**6**	table	доска объявлений	**13**	bulletin board	учительский стол	**18**	teacher's desk
компьютер	**7**	computer	громкоговорящая	**14**	P.A. system/	мусорное ведро	**19**	wastebasket
диаскопический	**8**	overhead	система оповещения/		loudspeaker			
проектор		projector	громкоговоритель					

ручка	**20**	pen	скоросшиватель/тетрадь	**27**	binder/notebook	маркер	**34**	marker
карандаш	**21**	pencil	бумага для скоросшивателя	**28**	notebook paper	кнопка	**35**	thumbtack
ластик	**22**	eraser	бумага в клетку	**29**	graph paper	клавиатура	**36**	keyboard
точилка	**23**	pencil sharpener	линейка	**30**	ruler	монитор	**37**	monitor
книга/учебник	**24**	book/textbook	калькулятор	**31**	calculator	мышка	**38**	mouse
рабочая тетрадь	**25**	workbook	мел	**32**	chalk	принтер	**39**	printer
тетрадь на пружине	**26**	spiral notebook	стиратель с доски	**33**	eraser			

A. Where's the **teacher**?
B. The **teacher** is *next to* the **board**.

A. Where's the **globe**?
B. The **globe** is *on* the **bookcase**.

A. Is there a/an _____ in your classroom?*
B. Yes. There's a/an _____
next to/on the _____ .

A. Is there a/an _____ in your classroom?*
B. No, there isn't.

Describe your classroom.
(There's a/an ....)

*With 28, 29, 32, use: Is there _____ in your classroom?

ЗАНЯТИЯ В КЛАССЕ

Назовите своё имя.	**1** Say your name.	Поднимите руку.	**16** Raise your hand.
Повторите своё имя.	**2** Repeat your name.	Задайте вопрос.	**17** Ask a question.
Произнесите имя по буквам.	**3** Spell your name.	Слушайте вопрос.	**18** Listen to the question.
Напишите своё имя (печатно).	**4** Print your name.	Ответьте на вопрос.	**19** Answer the question.
Распишитесь.	**5** Sign your name.	Слушайте ответ.	**20** Listen to the answer.
Встаньте.	**6** Stand up.	Сделайте домашнее задание.	**21** Do your homework.
Подойдите к доске.	**7** Go to the board.	Принесите домашнее задание.	**22** Bring in your homework.
Напишите на доске.	**8** Write on the board.	Проверьте ответы.	**23** Go over the answers.
Сотрите с доски.	**9** Erase the board.	Исправьте ошибки.	**24** Correct your mistakes.
Садитесь.	**10** Sit down./Take your seat.	Сдайте домашнее задание.	**25** Hand in your homework.
Откройте книгу.	**11** Open your book.	Совместно используйте книгу.	**26** Share a book.
Прочитайте страницу десять.	**12** Read page ten.	Обсудите вопрос.	**27** Discuss the question.
Выучите страницу десять.	**13** Study page ten.	Помогите друг другу.	**28** Help each other.
Закройте книгу.	**14** Close your book.	Работайте вместе.	**29** Work together.
Уберите книгу.	**15** Put away your book.	Поделитесь с классом.	**30** Share with the class.

Смотрите в словаре.	31 Look in the dictionary.	Раздайте тесты.	47 Pass out the tests.
Ищите слово.	32 Look up a word.	Ответьте на вопрос.	48 Answer the questions.
Произнесите слово.	33 Pronounce the word.	Проверьте свои ответы.	49 Check your answers.
Прочитайте значение.	34 Read the definition.	Соберите тесты.	50 Collect the tests.
Перепишите слово.	35 Copy the word.	Выберите правильный ответ.	51 Choose the correct answer.
Работайте самостоятельно.	36 Work alone./ Do your own work.	Обведите правильный ответ.	52 Circle the correct answer.
Работайте с партнёром.	37 Work with a partner.	Заполните пропущенное.	53 Fill in the blank.
Разделитесь на небольшие группы.	38 Break up into small groups.	Отметьте на листке с ответами./ Раскрасьте кружок с ответом.	54 Mark the answer sheet./ Bubble the answer.
Работайте в группе.	39 Work in a group.	Соедините подходящие слова.	55 Match the words.
Работайте всем классом.	40 Work as a class.	Подчеркните слово.	56 Underline the word.
Опустите шторы.	41 Lower the shades.	Зачеркните слово.	57 Cross out the word.
Выключите свет.	42 Turn off the lights.	Составьте слово.	58 Unscramble the word.
Смотрите на экран.	43 Look at the screen.	Поставьте слова в правильном порядке.	59 Put the words in order.
Конспектируйте./ Записывайте.	44 Take notes.	Напишите на отдельном листке бумаги.	60 Write on a separate sheet of paper.
Включите свет.	45 Turn on the lights.		
Достаньте листок бумаги.	46 Take out a piece of paper.		

You're the teacher! Give instructions to your students!

ПРЕДЛОГИ

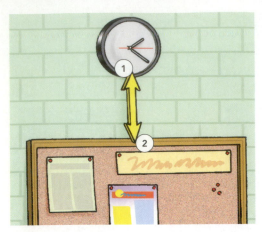
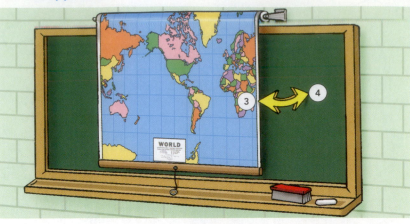
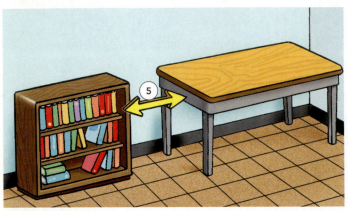
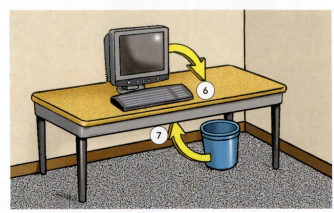
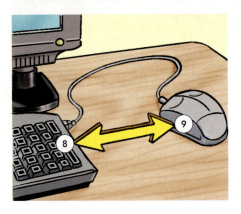

DICTIONARY

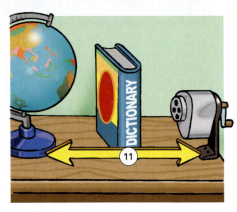

над	**1**	above	рядом с	**5**	next to	справа от	**9**	to the right of
под	**2**	below	на	**6**	on	в	**10**	in
перед	**3**	in front of	под	**7**	under	между	**11**	between
за	**4**	behind	слева от	**8**	to the left of			

[1–10]
A. Where's the *clock*?
B. The *clock* is **above** the
bulletin board.

[11]
A. Where's the *dictionary*?
B. The *dictionary* is **between** the
globe and the *pencil sharpener.*

Tell about the classroom on page 4. Use the prepositions in this lesson.   Tell about your classroom.

ПОВСЕДНЕВНЫЕ ДЕЛА I

вставать	**1**	get up	раздеваться	**11**	get undressed
принимать душ	**2**	take a shower	принимать ванную	**12**	take a bath
чистить зубы	**3**	brush *my** teeth	ложиться спать	**13**	go to bed
бриться	**4**	shave	спать	**14**	sleep
одеваться	**5**	get dressed	готовить завтрак	**15**	make breakfast
умываться	**6**	wash *my** face	готовить обед	**16**	make lunch
краситься	**7**	put on makeup	готовить ужин	**17**	cook / make dinner
расчёсываться	**8**	brush *my** hair	завтракать	**18**	eat / have breakfast
причёсываться	**9**	comb *my** hair	обедать	**19**	eat / have lunch
заправлять кровать	**10**	make the bed	ужинать	**20**	eat / have dinner

* my, his, her, our, your, their

A. What do you do every day?
B. **I get up**, **I take a shower**, and **I brush my teeth**.

A. What does he do every day?
B. He _____ s, he _____ s,
and he _____ s.

A. What does she do every day?
B. She _____ s, she _____ s,
and she _____ s.

What do you do every day? Make a list.

Interview some friends and tell about their everyday activities.

ПОВСЕДНЕВНЫЕ ДЕЛА II

убираться в квартире/ убираться в доме	**1**	clean the apartment/ clean the house
мыть посуду	**2**	wash the dishes
стирать	**3**	do the laundry
гладить	**4**	iron
кормить ребёнка	**5**	feed the baby
кормить кота	**6**	feed the cat
выгуливать собаку	**7**	walk the dog
учиться	**8**	study

идти на работу	**9**	go to work
идти в школу	**10**	go to school
ехать на работу	**11**	drive to work
ехать в школу на автобусе	**12**	take the bus to school
работать	**13**	work
уходить с работы	**14**	leave work
идти в магазин	**15**	go to the store
приходить домой	**16**	come home/get home

A. Hello. What are you doing?
B. I'm **clean**ing the **apartment**.

A. Hello, ... This is ....
   What are you doing?
B. I'm _____ing. How about you?
A. I'm _____ing.

A. Are you going to _____ soon?
B. Yes. I'm going to _____ in a little while.

What are you going to do tomorrow? Make a list of everything you are going to do.

НА ДОСУГЕ

смотреть телевизор	**1**	watch TV	играть на гитаре	**9**	play the guitar
слушать радио	**2**	listen to the radio	репетировать на пианино	**10**	practice the piano
слушать музыку	**3**	listen to music	заниматься спортом	**11**	exercise
читать книгу	**4**	read a book	плавать	**12**	swim
читать газету	**5**	read the newspaper	сажать цветы	**13**	plant flowers
играть	**6**	play	пользоваться компьютером	**14**	use the computer
играть в карты	**7**	play cards	писать письмо	**15**	write a letter
играть в баскетбол	**8**	play basketball	расслабляться	**16**	relax

A. Hi. What are you doing?
B. I'm **watch**ing **TV**.

A. Hi, ... Are you _____ing?
B. No, I'm not. I'm _____ing.

A. What's your (husband/wife/son/daughter/. . .) doing?
B. He's/She's _____ing.

What leisure activities do you like to do?

What do your family members and friends like to do?

ПОВСЕДНЕВНЫЕ РАЗГОВОРЫ

Greeting People   Приветствия

Leave Taking   Прощание

Здравствуйте./Привет.	**1**	Hello. / Hi.
Доброе утро.	**2**	Good morning.
Добрый день.	**3**	Good afternoon.
Добрый вечер.	**4**	Good evening.
Как ты?/	**5**	How are you?/
Как дела?		How are you doing?
Хорошо./Спасибо, хорошо./	**6**	Fine. / Fine, thanks. /
Нормально.		Okay.

Что нового?/	**7**	What's new?/
Что у тебя нового?		What's new with you?
Всё по-прежнему./	**8**	Not much. /
У меня всё по-прежнему.		Not too much.
До свидания./Пока.	**9**	Good-bye. / Bye.
До свидания.	**10**	Good night.
До встречи./	**11**	See you later. /
До скорого.		See you soon.

Introducing Yourself and Others   Представляться и Представлять Других

Getting Someone's Attention
Привлекать Чьё-то Внимание

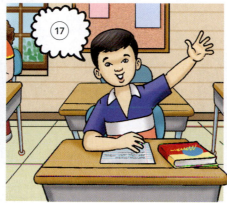

Expressing Gratitude
Выражать Благодарность

Saying You Don't Understand
Говорить что Вы не Понимаете

Calling Someone on the Telephone
Звонить Кому-то по Телефону

Здравствуйте.	**12**	Hello.
Меня зовут ..../		My name is ..../
Привет. Меня зовут		Hi. I'm ....
Мне тоже очень приятно./	**13**	Nice to meet you.
Взаимно. Мне тоже	**14**	Nice to meet you, too.
очень приятно.		
Познакомьтесь ..../	**15**	I'd like to introduce ..../
Это		This is ....
Извините.	**16**	Excuse me.
Можно вас спросить?	**17**	May I ask a question?
Спасибо.	**18**	Thank you. / Thanks.

Пожалуйста.	**19**	You're welcome.
Я не понимаю./	**20**	I don't understand. /
Извините. Я не понимаю.		Sorry. I don't understand.
Повторите пожалуйста.	**21**	Can you please repeat that?/
		Can you please say that again?
Здравствуйте. Это	**22**	Hello. This is ....
Могу я поговорить с ....?		May I please speak to ....?
Да, секундочку.	**23**	Yes. Hold on a moment.
Извините, ... сейчас нет.	**24**	I'm sorry. .... isn't here right now.

Practice conversations with other students. Use all the expressions on pages 12 and 13.

ПОГОДА

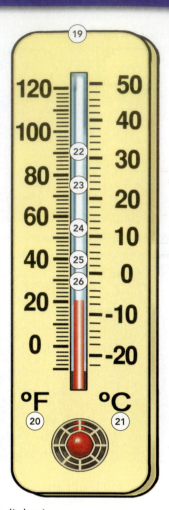

Погода	Weather			молния	**14**	lightning
солнечно	**1**	sunny		гроза	**15**	thunderstorm
облачно	**2**	cloudy		метель	**16**	snowstorm
ясно	**3**	clear		пыльная буря	**17**	dust storm
туманно	**4**	hazy		период сильной жары	**18**	heat wave
туманно	**5**	foggy				
смог в воздухе	**6**	smoggy		Температура		Temperature
ветрено	**7**	windy		градусник	**19**	thermometer
влажно	**8**	humid / muggy		Фаренгейт	**20**	Fahrenheit
идёт дождь	**9**	raining		Цельсий	**21**	Centigrade / Celsius
идёт мелкий дождь	**10**	drizzling		жарко	**22**	hot
идёт снег	**11**	snowing		тепло	**23**	warm
идёт град	**12**	hailing		прохладно	**24**	cool
идёт мокрый снег	**13**	sleeting		холодно	**25**	cold
				морозно	**26**	freezing

[1–13]
A. What's the weather like?
B. It's _____.

[14–18]
A. What's the weather forecast?
B. There's going to be ___[14]___/
a ___[15–18]___.

[20–26]
A. How's the weather?
B. It's ___[22–26]___.
A. What's the temperature?
B. It's . . . degrees ___[20–21]___.

What's the weather like today? What's the temperature?   What's the weather forecast for tomorrow?

ЦИФРЫ

Cardinal Numbers / Количественные Числительные

0 zero	**11** eleven	**21** twenty-one	**101** one hundred (and) one
1 one	**12** twelve	**22** twenty-two	**102** one hundred (and) two
2 two	**13** thirteen	**30** thirty	**1,000** one thousand
3 three	**14** fourteen	**40** forty	**10,000** ten thousand
4 four	**15** fifteen	**50** fifty	**100,000** one hundred thousand
5 five	**16** sixteen	**60** sixty	**1,000,000** one million
6 six	**17** seventeen	**70** seventy	**1,000,000,000** one billion
7 seven	**18** eighteen	**80** eighty	
8 eight	**19** nineteen	**90** ninety	
9 nine	**20** twenty	**100** one hundred	
10 ten			

A. How old are you?
B. I'm _____ years old.

A. How many people are there in your family?
B. _____.

Ordinal Numbers / Порядковые Числительные

1st first	**11th** eleventh	**21st** twenty-first	**101st** one hundred (and) first
2nd second	**12th** twelfth	**22nd** twenty-second	**102nd** one hundred (and) second
3rd third	**13th** thirteenth	**30th** thirtieth	**1,000th** one thousandth
4th fourth	**14th** fourteenth	**40th** fortieth	**10,000th** ten thousandth
5th fifth	**15th** fifteenth	**50th** fiftieth	**100,000th** one hundred thousandth
6th sixth	**16th** sixteenth	**60th** sixtieth	**1,000,000th** one millionth
7th seventh	**17th** seventeenth	**70th** seventieth	**1,000,000,000th** one billionth
8th eighth	**18th** eighteenth	**80th** eightieth	
9th ninth	**19th** nineteenth	**90th** ninetieth	
10th tenth	**20th** twentieth	**100th** one hundredth	

A. What floor do you live on?
B. I live on the _____ floor.

A. Is this your first trip to our country?
B. No. It's my _____ trip.

How many students are there in your class?

How many people are there in your country?

What were the names of your teachers in elementary school? (My *first*-grade teacher was Ms./Mrs./Mr. . . .)

two o'clock

*two fifteen /
a quarter after two*

*two thirty /
half past two*

*two forty-five
a quarter to three*

two oh five

*two twenty /
twenty after two*

*two forty /
twenty to three*

*two fifty-five
five to three*

A. What time is it?
B. It's _____.

A. What time does the movie begin?
B. At _____.

two A.M.

two P.M.

noon /
twelve noon

midnight /
twelve midnight

A. When does the train leave?
B. At _____.

A. What time will we arrive?
B. At _____.

Tell about your daily schedule:
 What do you do? When?
 (I get up at _____. I ....)

Do you usually have enough time to do things, or do you "run out of time"? Tell about it.

Tell about the use of time in different cultures or countries you know:
 Do people arrive on time for work? appointments? parties?
 Do trains and buses operate exactly on schedule?
 Do movies and sports events begin on time?
 Do workplaces use time clocks or timesheets to record employees' work hours?

Coins Монеты

ДЕНЬГИ

	Name	Value	Written as:	
1	penny	one cent	1¢	$ .01
2	nickel	five cents	5¢	$ .05
3	dime	ten cents	10¢	$ .10
4	quarter	twenty-five cents	25¢	$ .25
5	half dollar	fifty cents	50¢	$ .50
6	silver dollar	one dollar		$1.00

A. How much is a **penny** worth?
B. A **penny** is worth **one cent**.

A. *Soda* costs *ninety-five cents.* Do you have enough change?
B. Yes. I have a/two/three _____(s) and . . . .

Currency Купюры

	Name	We sometimes say:	Value	Written as:
7	(one-) dollar bill	a one	one dollar	$ 1.00
8	five-dollar bill	a five	five dollars	$ 5.00
9	ten-dollar bill	a ten	ten dollars	$ 10.00
10	twenty-dollar bill	a twenty	twenty dollars	$ 20.00
11	fifty-dollar bill	a fifty	fifty dollars	$ 50.00
12	(one-) hundred dollar bill	a hundred	one hundred dollars	$100.00

A. I'm going to the supermarket. Do you have any cash?
B. I have a **twenty-dollar bill**.
A. **Twenty dollars** is enough. Thanks.

A. Can you change a **five-dollar bill/a five**?
B. Yes. I have *five one-dollar bills/ five ones.*

Written as:	We say:
$1.30	a dollar and thirty cents / a dollar thirty
$2.50	two dollars and fifty cents / two fifty
$56.49	fifty-six dollars and forty-nine cents / fifty-six forty-nine

Tell about some things you usually buy. What do they cost?

Name and describe the coins and currency in your country. What are they worth in U.S. dollars?

КАЛЕНДАРЬ

год	1	year
месяц	2	month
неделя	3	week
день	4	day
выходные	5	weekend

Дни Недели Days of the Week

Воскресенье	6	Sunday
Понедельник	7	Monday
Вторник	8	Tuesday
Среда	9	Wednesday
Четверг	10	Thursday
Пятница	11	Friday
Суббота	12	Saturday

Месяца Года Months of the Year

Январь	13	January
Февраль	14	February
Март	15	March
Апрель	16	April
Май	17	May
Июнь	18	June
Июль	19	July
Август	20	August
Сентябрь	21	September
Октябрь	22	October
Ноябрь	23	November
Декабрь	24	December

3 Января 2012	25	January 3, 2012
		January third, two thousand twelve
день рождения	26	birthday
юбилей	27	anniversary
встреча	28	appointment

A. What year is it?
B. It's _____.

A. What's today's date?
B. It's _____.

[13–24]
A. What month is it?
B. It's _____.

[26–28]
A. When is your _____?
B. It's on _____.

[6–12]
A. What day is it?
B. It's _____.

Which days of the week do you
go to work/school?
(I go to work/school on _____.)

What do you do on the weekend?

What is your date of birth?
(I was born on ...*month day, year*....)

What's your favorite day of the week?
Why?

What's your favorite month of the
year? Why?

ВЫРАЖЕНИЯ ВРЕМЕНИ И СЕЗОНЫ

вчера	**1**	yesterday
сегодня	**2**	today
завтра	**3**	tomorrow
утро	**4**	morning
день	**5**	afternoon
вечер	**6**	evening
ночь	**7**	night
вчера утром	**8**	yesterday morning
вчера днём	**9**	yesterday afternoon
вчера вечером	**10**	yesterday evening

прошлой ночью	**11**	last night
сегодня утром	**12**	this morning
сегодня днём	**13**	this afternoon
сегодня вечером	**14**	this evening
сегодня ночью	**15**	tonight
завтра утром	**16**	tomorrow morning
завтра днём	**17**	tomorrow afternoon
завтра вечером	**18**	tomorrow evening
завтра ночью	**19**	tomorrow night
прошлая неделя	**20**	last week

текущая неделя	**21**	this week
следующая неделя	**22**	next week
раз в неделю	**23**	once a week
два раза в неделю	**24**	twice a week
три раза в неделю	**25**	three times a week
каждый день	**26**	every day

Сезоны Seasons

весна	**27**	spring
лето	**28**	summer
осень	**29**	fall/autumn
зима	**30**	winter

What did you do yesterday morning/afternoon/evening? What did you do last night?

What are you going to do tomorrow morning/afternoon/evening/night?

What did you do last week?

What are your plans for next week?

How many times a week do you have English class?/go to the supermarket?/exercise?

What's your favorite season? Why?

ВИДЫ ЖИЛЬЯ И РАЙОНЫ

жилой дом	**1** apartment building	приют	**9** shelter
дом	**2** house	ферма	**10** farm
двухквартирный дом	**3** duplex/two-family house	ферма	**11** ranch
коттедж	**4** townhouse/townhome	плавучий дом	**12** houseboat
кондоминиум	**5** condominium/condo	город	**13** the city
общежитие	**6** dormitory/dorm	пригород	**14** the suburbs
передвижной дом	**7** mobile home	деревня	**15** the country
дом (для) престарелых	**8** nursing home	городок/село/посёлок	**16** a town/village

A. Where do you live?

B. I live
- in a/an _____ [1–9] .
- on a _____ [10–12] .
- in _____ [13–16] .

[1–12]

A. Town Taxi Company.

B. Hello. Please send a taxi to
....(address).....

A. Is that a house or an apartment building?

B. It's a/an _____ .

A. All right. We'll be there right away.

[1–12]

A. This is the Emergency Operator.

B. Please send an ambulance to
....(address).....

A. Is that a private home?

B. It's a/an _____ .

A. What's your name and telephone number?

B. ....

Tell about people you know and where they live.

Discuss:

Who lives in dormitories?
Who lives in nursing homes?
Who lives in shelters?
Why?

книжный шкаф	**1**	bookcase	потолок	**11**	ceiling	диван/софа	**20** sofa/couch
фотография	**2**	picture/photograph	шторы	**12**	drapes	комнатное растение	**21** plant
картина	**3**	painting	окно	**13**	window	кофейный столик	**22** coffee table
каминная полка	**4**	mantel	диван	**14**	loveseat	коврик	**23** rug
камин	**5**	fireplace	стенка	**15**	wall unit	лампа	**24** lamp
каминная решётка	**6**	fireplace screen	динамик	**16**	speaker	абажур	**25** lampshade
DVD плеер	**7**	DVD player	музыкальный центр	**17**	stereo system	тумбочка	**26** end table
телевизор	**8**	television/TV	подставка для	**18**	magazine	пол	**27** floor
видеомагнитофон	**9**	VCR/video cassette	журналов		holder	торшер	**28** floor lamp
		recorder	декоративная	**19**	(throw) pillow	кресло	**29** armchair
стена	**10**	wall	подушка/думка				

A. Where are you?
B. I'm in the living room.
A. What are you doing?
B. I'm dusting* the **bookcase**.

* dusting/cleaning

A. You have a very nice living room!
B. Thank you.
A. Your _____ is/are beautiful!
B. Thank you for saying so.

A. Uh-oh! I just spilled coffee on your _____!
B. That's okay. Don't worry about it.

Tell about your living room.
(In my living room there's ....)

СТОЛОВАЯ КОМНАТА

обеденный стол	1	(dining room) table	салатница	13	salad bowl	
стул	2	(dining room) chair	блюдо	14	serving bowl	
буфет	3	buffet	блюдо	15	serving dish	
поднос	4	tray	ваза	16	vase	
заварочный чайник	5	teapot	свеча	17	candle	
кофейник	6	coffee pot	подсвечник	18	candlestick	
сахарница	7	sugar bowl	плоское блюдо	19	platter	
сливочник	8	creamer	маслёнка	20	butter dish	
кувшин	9	pitcher	солонка	21	salt shaker	
люстра	10	chandelier	перечница	22	pepper shaker	
шкаф для посуды	11	china cabinet	скатерть	23	tablecloth	
фарфор	12	china				

салфетка	24	napkin
вилка	25	fork
тарелка	26	plate
нож	27	knife
ложка	28	spoon
суповая тарелка	29	bowl
чашка/кружка	30	mug
стакан	31	glass
чашка	32	cup
блюдце	33	saucer

A. This **dining room table** is very nice.
B. Thank you. It was a gift from my *grandmother.**

*grandmother/grandfather/aunt/uncle/. . .

[In a store]
A. May I help you?
B. Yes, please. Do you have _____s?*
A. Yes. _____s* are right over there.
B. Thank you.

*With 12, use the singular.

[At home]
A. Look at this old _____ I just bought!
B. Where did you buy it?
A. At a yard sale. How do you like it?
B. It's VERY unusual!

Tell about your dining room.
(In my dining room there's
..............)

кровать	**1**	bed	жалюзи	**14**	blinds
спинка кровати	**2**	headboard	шторы	**15**	curtains
подушка	**3**	pillow	лампа	**16**	lamp
наволочка	**4**	pillowcase	будильник	**17**	alarm clock
простынь на резинке	**5**	fitted sheet	радио-часы	**18**	clock radio
простынь	**6**	(flat) sheet	тумбочка	**19**	night table/nightstand
одеяло	**7**	blanket	зеркало	**20**	mirror
одеяло с электроподогревом	**8**	electric blanket	шкатулка	**21**	jewelry box
юбка для кровати	**9**	dust ruffle	туалетный столик	**22**	dresser/bureau
покрывало	**10**	bedspread	матрац	**23**	mattress
одеяло	**11**	comforter/quilt	блок матрасных пружин	**24**	box spring
ковровое покрытие	**12**	carpet	корпус кровати	**25**	bed frame
комод	**13**	chest (of drawers)			

A. Ooh! Look at that big bug!
B. Where?
A. It's on the **bed**!
B. I'll get it.

[In a store]

A. Excuse me. I'm looking for a/an _____.*

B. We have some very nice _____s, and they're all on sale this week!

A. Oh, good!

* With 14 & 15, use: Excuse me. I'm looking for _____.

[In a bedroom]

A. Oh, no! I just lost my contact lens!

B. Where?

A. I think it's on the _____.

B. I'll help you look.

Tell about your bedroom.
(In my bedroom there's ....)

THE KITCHEN
КУХНЯ

холодильник	**1**	refrigerator	раковина	**12**	(kitchen) sink	плита	**24**	stove/range
морозильная камера	**2**	freezer	посудомоечная	**13**	dishwasher	конфорка	**25**	burner
мусорное ведро	**3**	garbage pail	машина			духовка	**26**	oven
(электрический)	**4**	(electric)	устройство для	**14**	(garbage)	тостер	**27**	toaster
миксер		mixer	переработки		disposal	кофеварка	**28**	coffeemaker
шкаф	**5**	cabinet	отходов в раковине			компактор	**29**	trash
держатель бумажных	**6**	paper towel	полотенце для	**15**	dish towel	мусора		compactor
полотенец		holder	посуды			разделочная	**30**	cutting
банка для сухих	**7**	canister	сушилка для	**16**	dish rack/	доска		board
продуктов			посуды		dish drainer	кулинарная	**31**	cookbook
столешница	**8**	(kitchen)	подставка для	**17**	spice rack	книга		
		counter	специй			кухонный	**32**	food
порошок для	**9**	dishwasher	электрооткрывалка	**18**	(electric) can	комбайн		processor
посудомоечной		detergent	консервных банок		opener	стул	**33**	kitchen chair
машины			блендер	**19**	blender	кухонный	**34**	kitchen
средство для	**10**	dishwashing	тостер/мини печь	**20**	toaster oven	стол		table
мытья посуды		liquid	микроволновая печь	**21**	microwave (oven)	салфетка-	**35**	placemat
(водопроводный)	**11**	faucet	прихватка	**22**	potholder	подставка		
кран			чайник	**23**	tea kettle			

A. I think we need a new **refrigerator**.
B. I think you're right.

[In a store]
A. Excuse me. Are your _____s still on sale?
B. Yes, they are. They're twenty percent off.

[In a kitchen]
A. When did you get this/these new _____(s)?
B. I got it/them last week.

Tell about your kitchen.
(In my kitchen there's ....)

ДЕТСКАЯ КОМНАТА

мишка	**1** teddy bear	погремушка	**17** rattle
радионяня	**2** baby monitor/intercom	ходунки	**18** walker
комод	**3** chest (of drawers)	колыбель	**19** cradle
детская кроватка	**4** crib	коляска	**20** stroller
мягкий бортик	**5** crib bumper/bumper pad	коляска	**21** baby carriage
подвесная игрушка для колыбели	**6** mobile	детское автокресло	**22** car seat/safety seat
пеленальный стол	**7** changing table	детское переносное устройство	**23** baby carrier
трикотажный комбинезон	**8** stretch suit	подогреватель пищи	**24** food warmer
матрац для пеленального стола	**9** changing pad	подставка для сиденья	**25** booster seat
ведро для подгузников	**10** diaper pail	детское сиденье	**26** baby seat
ночник	**11** night light	детский стульчик	**27** high chair
ящик для игрушек	**12** toy chest	передвижная кроватка	**28** portable crib
мягкая игрушка	**13** stuffed animal	горшок	**29** potty
кукла	**14** doll	кенгуру	**30** baby frontpack
качели	**15** swing	кенгуру	**31** baby backpack
(детский) манеж	**16** playpen		

A. Thank you for the **teddy bear**. It's a very nice gift.
B. You're welcome. Tell me, when are you due?
A. In a few more weeks.

A. That's a very nice _____. Where did you get it?
B. It was a gift from ....

A. Do you have everything you need before the baby comes?
B. Almost everything. We're still looking for a/an _____ and a/an _____.

Tell about your country:
What things do people buy for a new baby? Does a new baby sleep in a separate room, as in the United States?

ВАННАЯ КОМНАТА

мусорное ведро	**1**	wastebasket
гарнитур в	**2**	vanity
ванной комнате		
мыло	**3**	soap
мыльница	**4**	soap dish
ёмкость для	**5**	soap dispenser
жидкого мыла		
раковина	**6**	(bathroom) sink
кран	**7**	faucet
шкаф для лекарств	**8**	medicine cabinet
зеркало	**9**	mirror
стаканчик	**10**	cup
зубная щётка	**11**	toothbrush
подставка для	**12**	toothbrush
зубной щётки		holder
электрическая	**13**	electric
зубная щётка		toothbrush

фен	**14**	hair dryer
полка	**15**	shelf
корзина для	**16**	hamper
грязной одежды		
вентиляция	**17**	fan
банное полотенце	**18**	bath towel
полотенце для рук	**19**	hand towel
мочалка из	**20**	washcloth /
махровой ткани		facecloth
вешалка/держатель	**21**	towel rack
полотенец		
вантуз	**22**	plunger
ёршик для унитаза	**23**	toilet brush
туалетная бумага	**24**	toilet paper
освежитель воздуха	**25**	air freshener
унитаз	**26**	toilet
сиденье унитаза	**27**	toilet seat

душ	**28**	shower
верхний душ	**29**	shower head
занавеска для	**30**	shower
душа		curtain
ванна	**31**	bathtub / tub
резиновый	**32**	rubber
коврик		mat
стоковое	**33**	drain
отверстие		
губка	**34**	sponge
коврик для	**35**	bath mat
ванной		
весы	**36**	scale

A. Where's the **hair dryer**?
B. It's *on* the **vanity**.

A. Where's the **soap**?
B. It's *in* the **soap dish**.

A. Where's the **plunger**?
B. It's *next to* the **toilet brush**.

A. [Knock. Knock.] Did I leave my glasses in there?
B. Yes. They're on/in/next to the _____.

A. *Bobby*? You didn't clean up the bathroom! There's toothpaste on the _____, and there's powder all over the _____!
B. Sorry. I'll clean it up right away.

Tell about your bathroom. (In my bathroom there's ....)

Передний Двор	Front Yard		Задний Двор	Backyard	
фонарный столб	**1**	lamppost	лежак	**17**	lawn chair
почтовый ящик	**2**	mailbox	газонокосилка	**18**	lawnmower
дорожка	**3**	front walk	сарай (для инструментов)	**19**	tool shed
ступеньки	**4**	front steps	дверь-сетка	**20**	screen door
крыльцо	**5**	(front) porch	задняя дверь	**21**	back door
створка двери	**6**	storm door	дверная ручка	**22**	door knob
входная дверь	**7**	front door	терраса/крыльцо	**23**	deck
звонок	**8**	doorbell	гриль	**24**	barbecue/ (outdoor) grill
фонарь у входной двери	**9**	(front) light	патио	**25**	patio
окно	**10**	window	водосточный желоб	**26**	gutter
оконная сетка от насекомых	**11**	(window) screen	водосточная труба	**27**	drainpipe
ставни	**12**	shutter	спутниковая тарелка	**28**	satellite dish
крыша	**13**	roof	телевизионная антенна	**29**	TV antenna
гараж	**14**	garage	дымоход	**30**	chimney
ворота гаража	**15**	garage door	боковая дверь	**31**	side door
подъездная дорожка	**16**	driveway	забор	**32**	fence

A. When are you going to repair the **lamppost**?
B. I'm going to repair it next Saturday.

[On the telephone]
A. Harry's Home Repairs.
B. Hello. Do you fix _____s?
A. No, we don't.
B. Oh, okay. Thank you.

[At work on Monday morning]
A. What did you do this weekend?
B. Nothing much. I repaired my _____ and my _____.

Do you like to repair things?
What things can you repair yourself?
What things can't you repair? Who repairs them?

ЖИЛОЙ ДОМ

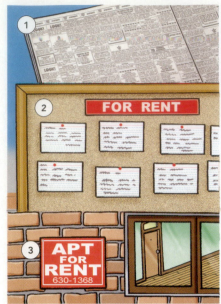

Искать Квартиру		**Looking for an Apartment**
квартирные объявления/ объявления	**1**	apartment ads/ classified ads
перечень квартирных объявлений	**2**	apartment listings
объявление-вывеска о сдаче жилья	**3**	vacancy sign

Подписывать Контракт		**Signing a Lease**
жилец	**4**	tenant
арендодатель	**5**	landlord
договор об аренде	**6**	lease
залог	**7**	security deposit

Въезжать		**Moving In**
грузовик/ фургон	**8**	moving truck/ moving van
сосед	**9**	neighbor
комендант	**10**	building manager
портье/швейцар	**11**	doorman
ключ	**12**	key
замок	**13**	lock
первый этаж	**14**	first floor
второй этаж	**15**	second floor
третий этаж	**16**	third floor
четвёртый этаж	**17**	fourth floor
крыша	**18**	roof
пожарная лестница	**19**	fire escape

автостоянка	**20**	parking garage
балкон	**21**	balcony
внутренний двор	**22**	courtyard
автостоянка	**23**	parking lot
место на автостоянке	**24**	parking space
бассейн	**25**	swimming pool
бассейн с гидромассажем	**26**	whirlpool
мусорный бак	**27**	trash bin
кондиционер воздуха	**28**	air conditioner

Вестибюль **Lobby**

домофон	**29**	intercom / speaker
звонок	**30**	buzzer
почтовый ящик	**31**	mailbox
лифт	**32**	elevator
лестница	**33**	stairway

Вход в Помещение **Doorway**

глазок	**34**	peephole
цепочка двери	**35**	(door) chain
замок	**36**	dead-bolt lock
индикатор/ датчик дыма	**37**	smoke detector

Коридор **Hallway**

пожарный выход/ запасной выход	**38**	fire exit / emergency stairway
пожарная сигнализация/сирена	**39**	fire alarm
автоматическая система пожаротушения	**40**	sprinkler system
управляющий	**41**	superintendent
мусоропровод	**42**	garbage chute / trash chute

Цокольный Этаж/Подвал **Basement**

чулан/кладовка	**43**	storage room
шкаф-кладовка	**44**	storage locker
помещение для стирки	**45**	laundry room
ограждение	**46**	security gate

[19–46]
A. Is there a **fire escape**?
B. Yes, there is. Do you want to see the apartment?
A. Yes, I do.

[19–46]
[Renting an apartment]
A. Let me show you around.
B. Okay.
A. This is the _____, and here's the _____.
B. I see.

[19–46]
[On the telephone]
A. Mom and Dad? I found an apartment.
B. Good. Tell us about it.
A. It has a/an _____ and a/an _____.
B. That's nice. Does it have a/an _____?
A. Yes, it does.

Do you or someone you know live in an apartment building? Tell about it.

ЖИЛИЩНЫЕ ПРОБЛЕМЫ И ИХ РЕШЕНИЕ

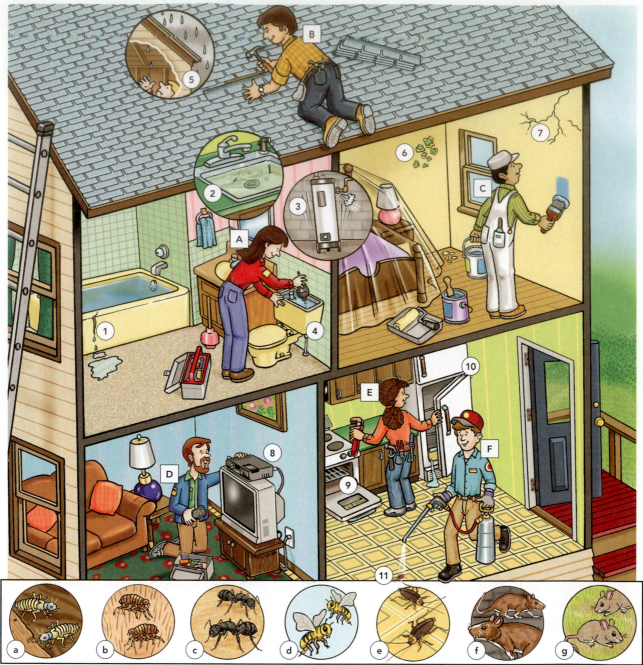

водопроводчик	**A**	**plumber**	**мастер по ремонту техники**	**E**	**appliance repairperson**

водопроводчик **A plumber**
Ванна протекает. **1** The bathtub is leaking.
Раковина засорилась. **2** The sink is clogged.
Обогреватель воды не работает. **3** The hot water heater isn't working.
Унитаз сломан. **4** The toilet is broken.

кровельщик **B roofer**
Крыша протекает. **5** The roof is leaking.

маляр **C (house) painter**
Краска отслаивается. **6** The paint is peeling.
Стена треснула. **7** The wall is cracked.

компания кабельного телевидения **D cable TV company**
Кабельное телевидение не работает. **8** The cable TV isn't working.

мастер по ремонту техники **E appliance repairperson**
Плита не работает. **9** The stove isn't working.
Холодильник сломан. **10** The refrigerator is broken.

специалист по дезинсекции **F exterminator/ pest control specialist**
____ на кухне. **11** There are ____ in the kitchen.
термиты **a** termites
блохи **b** fleas
муравьи **c** ants
пчёлы **d** bees
тараканы **e** cockroaches
крысы **f** rats
мыши **g** mice

| слесарь | **G locksmith** |
| Замок сломан. | **12** The lock is broken. |

электрик	**H electrician**
Фонарь у входной двери не включается.	**13** The front light doesn't go on.
Звонок не звонит.	**14** The doorbell doesn't ring.
Нет электричества в гостиной.	**15** The power is out in the living room.

| трубочист | **I chimneysweep** |
| Дымоход грязный. | **16** The chimney is dirty. |

| "мастер на все руки" | **J home repairperson/ "handyman"** |
| Кафель в ванной отваливается. | **17** The tiles in the bathroom are loose. |

плотник	**K carpenter**
Лестница сломана.	**18** The steps are broken.
Дверь не открывается.	**19** The door doesn't open.

сервис по системе отопления и кондиционирования воздуха	**L heating and air conditioning service**
Сломана система отопления.	**20** The heating system is broken.
Кондиционеры не работают.	**21** The air conditioning isn't working.

A. What's the matter?
B. ___[1–21]___.
A. I think we should call a/an ___[A–L]___.

[1–21]
A. I'm having a problem in my apartment/house.
B. What's the problem?
A. _____.

[A–L]
A. Can you recommend a good _____?
B. Yes. You should call ....

What do you do when there are problems in your home? Do you fix things yourself, or do you call someone?

УБОРКА ДОМА

подметать	**A**	sweep the floor
пылесосить	**B**	vacuum
мыть пол	**C**	mop the floor
мыть окна	**D**	wash the windows
пыль	**E**	dust
натирать пол воском	**F**	wax the floor
полировать мебель	**G**	polish the furniture
убираться в ванной комнате	**H**	clean the bathroom
выносить мусор	**I**	take out the garbage
веник/метла	**1**	broom
совок	**2**	dustpan
метёлка	**3**	whisk broom
щётка для чистки ковров	**4**	carpet sweeper
пылесос	**5**	vacuum (cleaner)
насадки для пылесоса	**6**	vacuum cleaner attachments
мешок для пылесоса	**7**	vacuum cleaner bag
ручной пылесос	**8**	hand vacuum

швабра	**9**	(dust) mop/(dry) mop
швабра	**10**	(sponge) mop
швабра	**11**	(wet) mop
бумажные полотенца	**12**	paper towels
средство для мытья окон	**13**	window cleaner
аммиак	**14**	ammonia
тряпка для вытирания пыли	**15**	dust cloth
метёлка из перьев для смахивания пыли	**16**	feather duster
мастика	**17**	floor wax
средство для полирования мебели	**18**	furniture polish
моющее средство	**19**	cleanser
жесткая щётка	**20**	scrub brush
губка	**21**	sponge
ведро	**22**	bucket/pail
мусорный бак	**23**	trash can/garbage can
мусорный бак для отходов на переработку	**24**	recycling bin

[A–I]
A. What are you doing?
B. I'm **sweep**ing **the floor**.

[1–24]
A. I can't find the **broom**.
B. Look over there!

[1–12, 15, 16, 20–24]
A. Excuse me. Do you sell _____(s)?
B. Yes. They're at the back of the store.
A. Thanks.

[13, 14, 17–19]
A. Excuse me. Do you sell _____?
B. Yes. It's at the back of the store.
A. Thanks.

What household cleaning chores do people do in your home? What things do they use?

ТОВАРЫ ПО ДОМУ

метр	**1**	yardstick	клеящая текстильная	**11**	duct tape	распылитель от	**19**	roach killer
мухобойка	**2**	fly swatter	лента			тараканов		
вантуз	**3**	plunger	батарейки	**12**	batteries	наждачная бумага	**20**	sandpaper
фонарь	**4**	flashlight	лампочки	**13**	lightbulbs/bulbs	краска	**21**	paint
удлинитель	**5**	extension cord	пробки	**14**	fuses	растворитель	**22**	paint thinner
рулетка	**6**	tape measure	масло	**15**	oil	кисть	**23**	paintbrush/
стремянка	**7**	step ladder	клей	**16**	glue			brush
мышеловка	**8**	mousetrap	рабочие перчатки	**17**	work gloves	лоток	**24**	paint pan
скотч	**9**	masking tape	распылитель от	**18**	bug spray/	валик	**25**	paint roller
изоляционная лента	**10**	electrical tape	насекомых		insect spray	распылитель красок	**26**	spray gun

A. I can't find the **yardstick**!
B. Look in the utility cabinet.
A. I did.
B. Oh! Wait a minute! I lent the **yardstick** to the neighbors.

[1–8, 23–26]

A. I'm going to the hardware store. Can you think of anything we need?
B. Yes. We need a/an _____.
A. Oh, that's right.

[9–22]

A. I'm going to the hardware store. Can you think of anything we need?
B. Yes. We need _____.
A. Oh, that's right.

What home supplies do you have? How and when do you use each one?

ИНСТРУМЕНТЫ

молоток	**1**	hammer	скребок	**12**	scraper	шлифовальный станок	**22**	power sander
резиновый молоток	**2**	mallet	устройство для зачистки проводов	**13**	wire stripper	фрезер	**23**	router
топор	**3**	ax	ручная дрель	**14**	hand drill	провод	**24**	wire
пила	**4**	saw/handsaw	тиски	**15**	vise	гвоздь	**25**	nail
ножовка	**5**	hacksaw	плоскогубцы	**16**	pliers	шайба	**26**	washer
нивелир	**6**	level	ящик для инструментов	**17**	toolbox	гайка	**27**	nut
отвёртка	**7**	screwdriver	рубанок	**18**	plane	шуруп	**28**	wood screw
крестообразная отвёртка	**8**	Phillips screwdriver	электродрель	**19**	electric drill	винт	**29**	machine screw
гаечный ключ	**9**	wrench	сверло	**20**	(drill) bit	болт	**30**	bolt
разводной гаечный ключ	**10**	monkey wrench/ pipe wrench	дисковая электропила/ электропила	**21**	circular saw/ power saw			
стамеска	**11**	chisel						

A. Can I borrow your **hammer**?
B. Sure.
A. Thanks.

* With 25–30, use: Could I borrow some _____s?

[1–15, 17–24]

A. Where's the _____?
B. It's on/next to/near/over/under the _____.

[16, 25–30]

A. Where are the _____s?
B. They're on/next to/near/over/under the _____.

Do you like to work with tools? What tools do you have in your home?

РАБОТА В САДУ И ИНСТРУМЕНТЫ

косить газон	**A** mow the lawn	газонокосилка	**1** lawnmower	сопло	**11** nozzle
сажать овощи	**B** plant vegetables	канистра с бензином	**2** gas can	пульверизатор	**12** sprinkler
сажать цветы	**C** plant flowers	триммер	**3** line trimmer	лейка	**13** watering can
поливать цветы	**D** water the flowers	лопата	**4** shovel	грабли	**14** rake
сгребать листья	**E** rake leaves	семена овощей	**5** vegetable seeds	воздуходув	**15** leaf blower
подстригать куст	**F** trim the hedge	тяпка/мотыга	**6** hoe	мешок для мусора	**16** yard waste bag
подрезать кусты	**G** prune the bushes	лопатка	**7** trowel	садовые ножницы	**17** (hedge) clippers
полоть	**H** weed	тачка	**8** wheelbarrow	шпалерные ножницы	**18** hedge trimmer
		удобрение	**9** fertilizer	секатор	**19** pruning shears
		шланг	**10** (garden) hose	инструмент для пропалывания	**20** weeder

[A–H]
A. Hi! Are you busy?
B. Yes. I'm **mow**ing **the lawn**.

[1–20]
A. What are you looking for?
B. The **lawnmower**.

[A–H]
A. What are you going to do tomorrow?
B. I'm going to _____.

[1–20]
A. Can I borrow your _____?
B. Sure.

Do you ever work with any of these tools? Which ones? What do you do with them?

МЕСТА В ГОРОДЕ I

булочная	**1**	bakery
банк	**2**	bank
парикмахерская	**3**	barber shop
книжный магазин	**4**	book store
автовокзал	**5**	bus station
кондитерская	**6**	candy store
агентство по продаже машин	**7**	car dealership
магазин открыток	**8**	card store
детский сад	**9**	child-care center / day-care center
химчистка	**10**	cleaners / dry cleaners
клиника	**11**	clinic
магазин одежды	**12**	clothing store
кафе/буфет	**13**	coffee shop
магазин по продаже компьютеров	**14**	computer store
магазин повседневного спроса	**15**	convenience store
копировальный центр	**16**	copy center

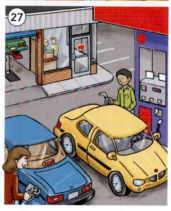

кулинария	**17**	delicatessen/deli		ресторан быстрого питания	**24**	fast-food restaurant
универмаг	**18**	department store		продавец цветов/цветочный магазин	**25**	flower shop/florist
магазин распродаж	**19**	discount store		мебельный магазин	**26**	furniture store
кафе	**20**	donut shop		бензоколонка/	**27**	gas station/
аптека	**21**	drug store/pharmacy		станция техобслуживания		service station
магазин электроники	**22**	electronics store		продуктовый магазин	**28**	grocery store
оптика/окулист	**23**	eye-care center/optician				

A. Where are you going?
B. I'm going to the **bakery**.

A. Hi! How are you today?
B. Fine. Where are you going?
A. To the _____. How about you?
B. I'm going to the _____.

A. Oh, no! I can't find my wallet/purse!
B. Did you leave it at the _____?
A. Maybe I did.

Which of these places are in your neighborhood?
(In my neighborhood there's a/an
..............)

МЕСТА В ГОРОДЕ II

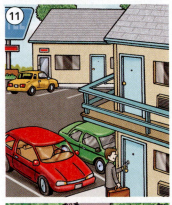

парикмахерская	**1**	hair salon
магазин инструментов	**2**	hardware store
фитнес центр	**3**	health club
больница	**4**	hospital
гостиница	**5**	hotel
кафе-мороженое	**6**	ice cream shop
ювелирный магазин	**7**	jewelry store
прачечная самообслуживания	**8**	laundromat

библиотека	**9**	library
магазин одежды для беременных	**10**	maternity shop
мотель	**11**	motel
кинотеатр	**12**	movie theater
магазин музыки	**13**	music store
маникюрный салон	**14**	nail salon
парк	**15**	park
магазин животных	**16**	pet shop/ pet store

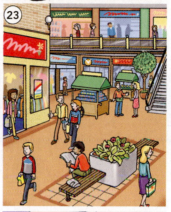

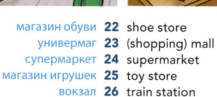

39

фотостудия	**17** photo shop
пиццерия	**18** pizza shop
почта	**19** post office
ресторан	**20** restaurant
школа	**21** school

магазин обуви	**22** shoe store
универмаг	**23** (shopping) mall
супермаркет	**24** supermarket
магазин игрушек	**25** toy store
вокзал	**26** train station

| туристическое агентство | **27** travel agency |
| магазин видео | **28** video store |

A. Where's the **hair salon**?
B. It's right over there.

A. Is there a/an _____ nearby?
B. Yes. There's a/an _____ around the corner.
A. Thanks.

A. Excuse me. Where's the _____?
B. It's down the street, next to the _____.
A. Thank you.

Which of these places are in your neighborhood?
(In my neighborhood there's a/an ....)

здание суда	**1**	courthouse	пожарный извещатель	**8**	fire alarm box	улица	**14** street
такси	**2**	taxi/cab/taxicab	почтовый ящик	**9**	mailbox	фонарь	**15** street light
стоянка такси	**3**	taxi stand	водоотвод/ сточное отверстие	**10**	sewer	автостоянка	**16** parking lot
таксист	**4**	taxi driver/ cab driver	полицейский участок	**11**	police station	контролёр парковки	**17** meter maid
пожарный гидрант	**5**	fire hydrant	тюрьма	**12**	jail	автомат для оплаты парковки	**18** parking meter
мусорный бак	**6**	trash container	тротуар	**13**	sidewalk	мусоровоз	**19** garbage truck
здание мэрии	**7**	city hall				метро	**20** subway
						станция метро	**21** subway station

газетный киоск	**22**	newsstand		автобусная остановка	**32**	bus stop
светофор	**23**	traffic light / traffic signal		автобус	**33**	bus
				водитель автобуса	**34**	bus driver
перекрёсток	**24**	intersection		офисный центр	**35**	office building
полицейский	**25**	police officer		телефон-автомат	**36**	public telephone
пешеходный переход	**26**	crosswalk		указатель улицы	**37**	street sign
пешеход	**27**	pedestrian		люк	**38**	manhole
машина с мороженым	**28**	ice cream truck		мотоцикл	**39**	motorcycle
бордюр	**29**	curb		уличный торговец	**40**	street vendor
автостоянка	**30**	parking garage		окно обслуживания автомобилей	**41**	drive-through window
пожарная станция	**31**	fire station				

A. Where's the _____?
B. On / In / Next to / Between / Across from / In front of / Behind / Under / Over the _____.

[An Election Speech]

If I am elected mayor, I'll take care of all the problems in our city. We need to do something about our _____s. We also need to do something about our _____s. And look at our _____s! We REALLY need to do something about THEM! We need a new mayor who can solve these problems. If I am elected mayor, we'll be proud of our _____s, _____s, and _____s again! Vote for me!

Go to an intersection in your city or town. What do you see? Make a list. Then tell about it.

ЛЮДИ И ИХ ОПИСАНИЕ

ребёнок-дети	**1**	**child-children**
младенец	**2**	baby/infant
ребёнок	**3**	toddler
мальчик	**4**	boy
девочка	**5**	girl
подросток	**6**	teenager
взрослый	**7**	**adult**
мужчина–мужчины	**8**	man–men
женщина–женщины	**9**	woman–women
пожилой человек	**10**	senior citizen/ elderly person

возраст	**age**	
молодой	**11**	young
среднего возраста	**12**	middle-aged
старый/пожилой	**13**	old/elderly
рост	**height**	
высокий	**14**	tall
среднего роста	**15**	average height
низкий/невысокий	**16**	short
вес	**weight**	
крупный/полный	**17**	heavy
среднего телосложения	**18**	average weight
худой/стройный	**19**	thin/slim
беременная	**20**	pregnant

физически неполноценный	**21**	physically challenged
с проблемой зрения	**22**	vision impaired
с проблемой слуха	**23**	hearing impaired

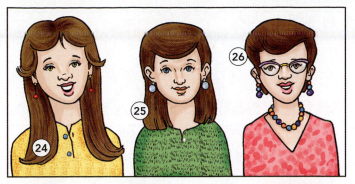

Описание Волос		Describing Hair
длинные	**24**	long
по плечи	**25**	shoulder length
короткие	**26**	short
прямые	**27**	straight
волнистые	**28**	wavy
кудрявые	**29**	curly
чёрные	**30**	black

русые	**31**	brown
светлые	**32**	blond
рыжие	**33**	red
седые	**34**	gray
лысый	**35**	bald
борода	**36**	beard
усы	**37**	mustache

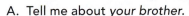

A. Tell me about *your brother*.
B. *He's a tall heavy boy* with *short curly brown* hair.

A. What does *your new boss* look like?
B. *She's average height*, and *she* has *long straight black* hair.

A. Can you describe *the person*?
B. *He's a tall thin middle-aged man.*
A. Anything else?
B. Yes. *He's bald*, and *he* has *a mustache.*

A. Can you describe *your grandmother*?
B. *She's a short thin elderly person* with *long wavy gray* hair.
A. Anything else?
B. Yes. *She's hearing impaired.*

Tell about yourself.

Tell about people in your family.

Tell about your favorite actor or actress or other famous person.

ОПИСАНИЕ ЛЮДЕЙ И ВЕЩЕЙ

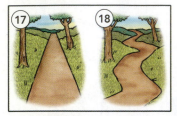

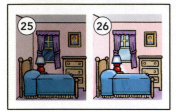

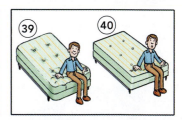

новый – старый	**1–2**	new – old
молодой – старый	**3–4**	young – old
высокий – низкий	**5–6**	tall – short
длинный – короткий	**7–8**	long – short
большой – маленький	**9–10**	large/big – small/little
быстрый – медленный	**11–12**	fast – slow
толстый – худой	**13–14**	heavy/fat – thin/skinny
тяжёлый – лёгкий	**15–16**	heavy – light
прямой – извилистый	**17–18**	straight – crooked
прямой – кудрявый	**19–20**	straight – curly
широкий – узкий	**21–22**	wide – narrow
толстый – тонкий	**23–24**	thick – thin

темно – светло	**25–26**	dark – light
высоко – низко	**27–28**	high – low
свободно – тесно	**29–30**	loose – tight
хорошо – плохо	**31–32**	good – bad
горячо – холодно	**33–34**	hot – cold
аккуратно – беспорядочно	**35–36**	neat – messy
чисто – грязно	**37–38**	clean – dirty
мягко – жёстко	**39–40**	soft – hard
легко – трудно/тяжело	**41–42**	easy – difficult/hard
гладко – грубо	**43–44**	smooth – rough
шумно/громко – тихо	**45–46**	noisy/loud – quiet
замужем/женат – не замужем/холост	**47–48**	married – single

  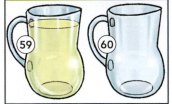 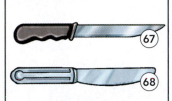

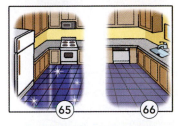   

богатый – бедный	**49–50** rich/wealthy – poor	нарядный – простой	**63–64** fancy – plain
красивая – уродливая	**51–52** pretty/beautiful – ugly	блестящий – тусклый	**65–66** shiny – dull
красивый – уродливый	**53–54** handsome – ugly	острый – тупой	**67–68** sharp – dull
мокрый – сухой	**55–56** wet – dry	удобный – неудобный	**69–70** comfortable – uncomfortable
открыто – закрыто	**57–58** open – closed	честный – нечестный	**71–72** honest – dishonest
полный – пустой	**59–60** full – empty		
дорогой – дешёвый/ недорогой	**61–62** expensive – cheap/ inexpensive		

[1–2]
A. Is your car **new**?
B. No. It's **old**.

1–2	Is your car _____?	25–26	Is the room _____?	49–50	Is your uncle _____?
3–4	Is he _____?	27–28	Is the bridge _____?	51–52	Is the witch _____?
5–6	Is your sister _____?	29–30	Are the pants _____?	53–54	Is the pirate _____?
7–8	Is his hair _____?	31–32	Are your neighbor's children _____?	55–56	Are the clothes _____?
9–10	Is their dog _____?	33–34	Is the water _____?	57–58	Is the door _____?
11–12	Is the train _____?	35–36	Is your desk _____?	59–60	Is the pitcher _____?
13–14	Is your friend _____?	37–38	Are the windows _____?	61–62	Is that restaurant _____?
15–16	Is the box _____?	39–40	Is the mattress _____?	63–64	Is the dress _____?
17–18	Is the road _____?	41–42	Is the homework _____?	65–66	Is your kitchen floor _____?
19–20	Is her hair _____?	43–44	Is your skin _____?	67–68	Is the knife _____?
21–22	Is the tie _____?	45–46	Is your neighbor _____?	69–70	Is the chair _____?
23–24	Is the line _____?	47–48	Is your sister _____?	71–72	Is he _____?

A. Tell me about your ....
B. He's/She's/It's/They're _____.

A. Do you have a/an _____ ....?
B. No. I have a/an _____ ....

Describe yourself.

Describe a person you know.

Describe some things in your home.

Describe some things in your community.

уставший	**1**	tired	голодный	**7**	hungry	печальный	**12**	miserable
сонный	**2**	sleepy	испытываемый жаждой	**8**	thirsty	возбуждённый	**13**	excited
обессиленный	**3**	exhausted	сытый	**9**	full	разочарованный	**14**	disappointed
больной	**4**	sick/ill	счастливый	**10**	happy	расстроенный	**15**	upset
жарко	**5**	hot	грустный/ несчастный	**11**	sad/unhappy	раздражённый	**16**	annoyed
замерзший	**6**	cold						

злой	**17** angry/mad	одинокий	**23** lonely	скучающий	**28** bored
яростный	**18** furious	тоскующий по дому/ по родине	**24** homesick	гордый	**29** proud
чувствующий отвращение	**19** disgusted	нервничающий	**25** nervous	смущённый/ стыдящийся	**30** embarrassed
разочарованный	**20** frustrated	озабоченный/ волнующийся	**26** worried	завидующий	**31** jealous
удивлённый	**21** surprised	испуганный/боящийся	**27** scared/afraid	смущённый/ сбитый с толку	**32** confused
потрясённый	**22** shocked				

A. You look _____.
B. I am. I'm VERY _____.

A. Are you _____?
B. No. Why do you ask? Do I LOOK _____?
A. Yes. You do.

What makes you happy? sad? mad?

What do you do when you feel nervous? annoyed?

Do you ever feel embarrassed? When?

ФРУКТЫ

яблоко	**1**	apple	инжир	**12**	fig	апельсин	**22**	orange
персик	**2**	peach	кокос	**13**	coconut	мандарин	**23**	tangerine
груша	**3**	pear	авокадо	**14**	avocado	виноград	**24**	grapes
банан	**4**	banana	мускусная дыня	**15**	cantaloupe	вишня/черешня	**25**	cherries
овощной банан	**5**	plantain	зимняя дыня	**16**	honeydew (melon)	чернослив	**26**	prunes
слива	**6**	plum	арбуз	**17**	watermelon	финики	**27**	dates
абрикос	**7**	apricot	ананас	**18**	pineapple	изюм	**28**	raisins
нектарин	**8**	nectarine	грейпфрут	**19**	grapefruit	орехи	**29**	nuts
киви	**9**	kiwi	лимон	**20**	lemon	малина	**30**	raspberries
папайя	**10**	papaya	лайм	**21**	lime	черника	**31**	blueberries
манго	**11**	mango				клубника	**32**	strawberries

[1–23]
A. This **apple** is delicious! Where did you get it?
B. At *Sam's Supermarket*.

[24–32]
A. These **grapes** are delicious! Where did you get them?
B. At *Franny's Fruit Stand*.

A. I'm hungry. Do we have any fruit?
B. Yes. We have _____s* and _____s.*

A. Do we have any more _____s?†
B. No. I'll get some more when I go to the supermarket.

What are your favorite fruits?
Which fruits don't you like?

Which of these fruits grow where you live?

Name and describe other fruits you know.

* With 15–19, use:
  We have _____ and _____.

† With 15–19, use:
  Do we have any more _____?

ОВОЩИ

сельдерей	**1** celery	горох	**16** pea	батат/сладкий	**29** sweet potato
кукуруза	**2** corn	стручковая фасоль/	**17** string bean/	картофель	
брокколи	**3** broccoli	зелёная фасоль	green bean	ямс	**30** yam
цветная капуста	**4** cauliflower	лимская фасоль	**18** lima bean	зелёный перец/	**31** green pepper/
шпинат	**5** spinach	чёрная фасоль	**19** black bean	сладкий перец	sweet pepper
петрушка	**6** parsley	фасоль	**20** kidney bean	красный/	**32** red pepper
спаржа	**7** asparagus	брюссельская	**21** brussels	болгарский перец	
баклажан	**8** eggplant	капуста	sprout	острый зелёный	**33** jalapeño
салат	**9** lettuce	огурец	**22** cucumber	перец	(pepper)
капуста	**10** cabbage	помидор	**23** tomato	острый красный перец	**34** chili pepper
китайская капуста	**11** bok choy	морковь	**24** carrot	свёкла	**35** beet
цукини/кабачок	**12** zucchini	редиска	**25** radish	лук	**36** onion
кабачок	**13** acorn squash	гриб	**26** mushroom	зелёный лук	**37** scallion/
кабачок	**14** butternut squash	артишок	**27** artichoke		green onion
чеснок	**15** garlic	картошка	**28** potato	репа	**38** turnip

A. What do we need from the supermarket?
B. We need **celery*** and **peas**.†

* 1–15   † 16–38

A. How do you like the
___[1–15]___ / ___[16–38]___s?
B. It's/They're delicious.

A. *Bobby*? Finish your vegetables!
B. But you KNOW I hate
___[1–15]___ / ___[16–38]___s!
A. I know. But it's/they're good for you!

Which vegetables do you like?
Which vegetables don't you like?

Which of these vegetables grow where you live?

Name and describe other vegetables you know.

МЯСО, ПТИЦА И МОРЕПРОДУКТЫ

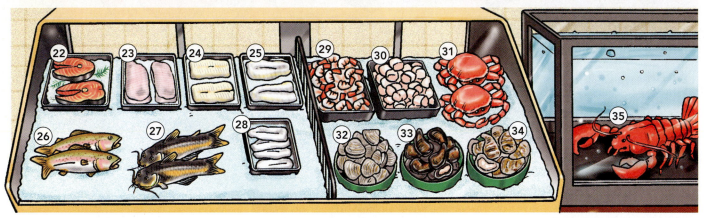

Мясо	Meat		Птица	Poultry				
стейк	**1** steak		курица	**15** chicken		мелкая камбала	**25** flounder
фарш говяжий	**2** ground beef		куриные грудки	**16** chicken breasts		форель	**26** trout
мясо для жаркого	**3** stewing beef		куриные ножки/	**17** chicken legs/		сом	**27** catfish
ростбиф	**4** roast beef		куриные голени	drumsticks		филе палтуса/	**28** filet of
рёбра	**5** ribs		куриные крылышки	**18** chicken wings		камбалы	sole
баранья нога	**6** leg of lamb		куриные бёдра	**19** chicken thighs		**МОЛЛЮСКИ И**	**SHELLFISH**
стейки из ягнёнка	**7** lamb chops		индейка	**20** turkey		**РАКООБРАЗНЫЕ**	
брюшина	**8** tripe		утка	**21** duck		креветки	**29** shrimp
печень	**9** liver					гребешки	**30** scallops
свинина	**10** pork		**Морепродукты**	**Seafood**		краб	**31** crabs
стейки из свинины	**11** pork chops		РЫБА	FISH		моллюски	**32** clams
колбаски для жарки	**12** sausages		лосось/сёмга	**22** salmon		мидии	**33** mussels
ветчина	**13** ham		палтус	**23** halibut		устрицы	**34** oysters
бекон	**14** bacon		пикша	**24** haddock		омар	**35** lobster

A. I'm going to the supermarket. What do we need?
B. Please get some **steak**.
A. **Steak**? All right.

A. Excuse me. Where can I find _____?
B. Look in the _____ Section.
A. Thank you.

A. This/These _____ looks/
look very fresh!
B. Let's get some for dinner.

Do you eat meat, poultry, or seafood?
Which of these foods do you like?

Which of these foods are popular in your country

МОЛОЧНЫЕ ПРОДУКТЫ, СОКИ И НАПИТКИ

Молочные Продукты	Dairy Products		
молоко	**1**	milk	
молоко с низким содержанием жира	**2**	low-fat milk	
обезжиренное молоко	**3**	skim milk	
шоколадное молоко	**4**	chocolate milk	
апельсиновый сок	**5**	orange juice*	
сыр	**6**	cheese	
масло	**7**	butter	
маргарин	**8**	margarine	
сметана	**9**	sour cream	
сливочный сыр	**10**	cream cheese	
творог	**11**	cottage cheese	
йогурт	**12**	yogurt	
тофу*	**13**	tofu*	
яйца	**14**	eggs	

Соки	Juices	
яблочный сок	**15**	apple juice
ананасовый сок	**16**	pineapple juice
грейпфрутовый сок	**17**	grapefruit juice
томатный сок	**18**	tomato juice
виноградный сок	**19**	grape juice
фруктовый напиток/пунш	**20**	fruit punch
упаковка порций сока	**21**	juice paks
сухой концентрат фруктового напитка	**22**	powdered drink mix

Bwason	Beverages	
газированный напиток	**23**	soda
газированный напиток с заменителем сахара	**24**	diet soda
вода	**25**	bottled water

Кофе и Чай	Coffee and Tea	
кофе	**26**	coffee
кофе без кофеина	**27**	decaffeinated coffee/decaf
растворимый кофе	**28**	instant coffee
чай	**29**	tea
травяной чай	**30**	herbal tea
какао/смесь для горячего шоколада	**31**	cocoa/hot chocolate mix

* Апельсиновый сок и тофу не относятся к молочным продуктам, но обычно находятся в этом отделе.

A. I'm going to the supermarket to get some **milk**.
Do we need anything else?
B. Yes. Please get some **apple juice**.

A. Excuse me. Where can I find _____?
B. Look in the _____ Section.
A. Thanks.

A. Look! _____ is/are on sale this week!
B. Let's get some!

Which of these foods do you like?

Which of these foods are good for you?

Which brands of these foods do you buy?

КОЛБАСНО-СЫРНЫЙ ОТДЕЛ, ЗАМОРОЖЕННЫЕ ПРОДУКТЫ И ЗАКУСКИ

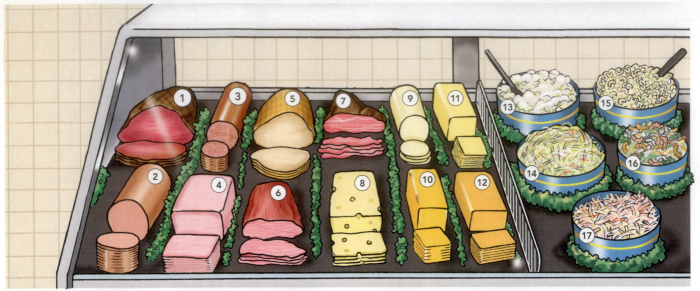

Колбасно-Сырный Отдел		Deli
ростбиф	**1**	roast beef
болонская/докторская колбаса	**2**	bologna
салями	**3**	salami
ветчина	**4**	ham
индейка	**5**	turkey
солонина	**6**	corned beef
пастрами/копчёная говядина	**7**	pastrami
швейцарский сыр	**8**	Swiss cheese
проволоне	**9**	provolone
американский сыр	**10**	American cheese
моцарелла	**11**	mozzarella
сыр чеддер	**12**	cheddar cheese
картофельный салат	**13**	potato salad
капустный салат	**14**	cole slaw
макаронный салат	**15**	macaroni salad
макаронный салат	**16**	pasta salad
салат из морепродуктов	**17**	seafood salad

Замороженные Продукты		Frozen Foods
мороженое	**18**	ice cream
замороженные овощи	**19**	frozen vegetables
полуфабрикаты	**20**	frozen dinners
замороженный лимонный напиток	**21**	frozen lemonade
замороженный апельсиновый сок	**22**	frozen orange juice

Закуски		Snack Foods
картофельные чипсы	**23**	potato chips
кукурузные чипсы	**24**	tortilla chips
крендельки	**25**	pretzels
орехи	**26**	nuts
попкорн	**27**	popcorn

A. Should we get some **roast beef**?
B. Good idea. And let's get some **potato salad**.

[1–17]
A. May I help you?
B. Yes, please. I'd like some _____.

[1–27]
A. Excuse me. Where is/are _____?
B. It's/They're in the _____ Section.

What kinds of snack foods are popular in your country?

Are frozen foods common in your country? What kinds of foods are in the Frozen Foods Section?

ПРОДУКТЫ

Фасованные Товары	**Packaged Goods**	арахисовое масло	**14** peanut butter
хлопья из круп	**1** cereal		
печенье	**2** cookies	**Соусы**	**Condiments**
крекеры	**3** crackers	кетчуп	**15** ketchup
макароны	**4** macaroni	горчица	**16** mustard
лапша	**5** noodles	соус из маринованных огурцов	**17** relish
спагетти	**6** spaghetti	маринованные огурцы	**18** pickles
рис	**7** rice	оливки	**19** olives
		соль	**20** salt
Консервы	**Canned Goods**	перец	**21** pepper
суп	**8** soup	приправы	**22** spices
тунец	**9** tuna (fish)	соевый соус	**23** soy sauce
консервированные овощи	**10** (canned) vegetables	майонез	**24** mayonnaise
консервированные фрукты	**11** (canned) fruit	растительное масло	**25** (cooking) oil
		оливковое масло	**26** olive oil
Варенье и Джемы	**Jams and Jellies**	острый мексиканский соус	**27** salsa
варенье	**12** jam		
джем	**13** jelly		

уксус	**28** vinegar
заправка для салата	**29** salad dressing
Хлебобулочные Изделия	**Baked Goods**
хлеб	**30** bread
булочки	**31** rolls
сдобная пышка	**32** English muffins
пита	**33** pita bread
торт	**34** cake
Продукты для Выпечки	**Baking Products**
мука	**35** flour
сахар	**36** sugar
смесь для торта	**37** cake mix

A. I got **cereal** and **soup**. What else is on the shopping list?
B. **Ketchup** and **bread**.

A. Excuse me. I'm looking for _____.
B. It's/They're next to the _____.

A. Pardon me. I'm looking for _____.
B. It's/They're between the _____ and the _____.

Which of these foods do you like?

Which brands of these foods do you buy?

ХОЗЯЙСТВЕННЫЕ ТОВАРЫ, ДЕТСКИЕ ТОВАРЫ И КОРМ ДЛЯ ЖИВОТНЫХ

Товары из Бумаги	Paper Products		жидкое мыло	11	liquid soap
салфетка	1 napkins		алюминиевая фольга	12	aluminum foil
бумажные стаканчики	2 paper cups		пищевая плёнка	13	plastic wrap
салфетки носовые	3 tissues		вощёная бумага	14	waxed paper
соломка для напитков	4 straws				
бумажные тарелки	5 paper plates		**Детские Товары**		**Baby Products**
бумажные полотенца	6 paper towels		детская каша	15	baby cereal
туалетная бумага	7 toilet paper		детское питание	16	baby food
			детская молочная смесь	17	formula
Хозяйственные Товары	**Household Items**		влажные салфетки	18	wipes
мешочки для бутербродов/ сэндвичей	8 sandwich bags		подгузники	19	(disposable) diapers
			Корм для Животных		**Pet Food**
мешки для мусора	9 trash bags		корм для кошек	20	cat food
мыло	10 soap		корм для собак	21	dog food

A. Excuse me. Where can I find **napkins**?
B. **Napkins**? Look in Aisle 4.

[7, 10–17, 20, 21]

A. We forgot to get _____!

B. I'll get it. Where is it?

A. It's in Aisle _____.

[1–6, 8, 9, 18, 19]

A. We forgot to get _____!

B. I'll get them. Where are they?

A. They're in Aisle _____.

What do you need from the supermarket?
Make a complete shopping list!

СУПЕРМАРКЕТ

проход/ряд	**1**	aisle	экспресс-касса	**15**	express checkout (line)
покупатель/клиент	**2**	shopper/customer	бульварная пресса	**16**	tabloid (newspaper)
корзина для покупок	**3**	shopping basket	журнал	**17**	magazine
очередь	**4**	checkout line	сканер	**18**	scanner
касса	**5**	checkout counter	пластиковый пакет	**19**	plastic bag
ленточный конвейер	**6**	conveyor belt	сельскохозяйственные продукты	**20**	produce
кассовый аппарат	**7**	cash register	заведующий магазином	**21**	manager
тележка для покупок	**8**	shopping cart	сотрудник магазина	**22**	clerk
жевательная резинка	**9**	(chewing) gum	весы	**23**	scale
конфеты	**10**	candy	автомат приёма тары для вторичной переработки жести	**24**	can-return machine
купоны	**11**	coupons	автомат приёма тары для вторичной переработки бутылок	**25**	bottle-return machine
кассир	**12**	cashier			
бумажный пакет	**13**	paper bag			
упаковщик	**14**	bagger/packer			

[1–8, 11–19, 21–25]
A. This is a gigantic supermarket!
B. It is! Look at all the **aisle**s!

[9, 10, 20]
A. This is a gigantic supermarket!
B. It is. Look at all the **produce**!

Where do you usually shop for food? Do you go to a supermarket, or do you go to a small grocery store? Describe the place where you shop.

Describe the differences between U.S. supermarkets and food stores in your country.

CONTAINERS AND QUANTITIES

ЁМКОСТИ И КОЛИЧЕСТВА

пакет **1** bag	кочан **9** head	мера сливочного масла **16** stick
бутылка **2** bottle	банка **10** jar	тюбик **17** tube
коробка **3** box	батон– батоны **11** loaf–loaves	пинта **18** pint
связка/пучок **4** bunch	упаковка/пачка **12** pack	кварта **19** quart
консервная банка **5** can	пакет/упаковка **13** package	пол галлона **20** half-gallon
картонная упаковка **6** carton	рулон **14** roll	галлон **21** gallon
контейнер **7** container	упаковка по шесть **15** six-pack	литр **22** liter
дюжина **8** dozen*		фунт **23** pound

* "a dozen eggs," не "a dozen of eggs"

A. Please get a **bag** of *flour* when you go to the supermarket.
B. A **bag** of *flour*? Okay.

A. Please get two **bottles** of *ketchup* when you go to the supermarket.
B. Two **bottles** of *ketchup*? Okay.

[At home]
A. What did you get at the supermarket?
B. I got _____, _____, and _____.

[In a supermarket]
A. Is this the express checkout line?
B. Yes, it is. Do you have more than eight items?
A. No. I only have _____, _____, and _____.

Open your kitchen cabinets and refrigerator. Make a list of all the things you find.

What do you do with empty bottles, jars, and cans? Do you recycle them, reuse them, or throw them away?

ЕДИНИЦЫ ИЗМЕРЕНИЯ

| чайная ложка | teaspoon
tsp. | столовая ложка | tablespoon
Tbsp. | жидкая унция | 1 (fluid) ounce
1 fl. oz. |

стакан cup
c.
8 fl. ozs.

пинта pint
pt.
16 fl. ozs.

кварта quart
qt.
32 fl. ozs.

галлон gallon
gal.
128 fl. ozs.

A. How much water should I put in?
B. The recipe says to add one _____ of water.

A. This fruit punch is delicious! What's in it?
B. Two _____s of apple juice, three _____s of orange juice, and a _____ of grape juice.

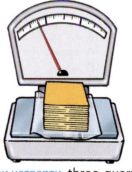

унция an ounce

oz.

**четверть
фунта** a quarter
of a pound
1/4 lb.
4 ozs.

полфунта half a
pound
1/2 lb.
8 ozs.

**три четверти
фунта** three-quarters
of a pound
3/4 lb.
12 ozs.

фунт a pound

lb.
16 ozs.

A. How much roast beef would you like?
B. I'd like _____, please.
A. Anything else?
B. Yes. Please give me _____ of Swiss cheese.

A. This chili tastes very good! What did you put in it?
B. _____ of ground beef, _____ of beans, _____ of tomatoes, and _____ of chili powder.

FOOD PREPARATION AND RECIPES
ПРИГОТОВЛЕНИЕ ПИЩИ И РЕЦЕПТЫ

шинковать	**1**	cut (up)
порубить	**2**	chop (up)
нарезать	**3**	slice
натереть	**4**	grate
почистить	**5**	peel
разбить	**6**	break
взбить	**7**	beat
помешать	**8**	stir
влить	**9**	pour
добавить	**10**	add
смешать ____ и ____	**11**	combine ____ and ____
перемешать ____ и ____	**12**	mix ____ and ____
поставить ____ в ____	**13**	put ____ in ____

готовить	**14**	cook
выпекать	**15**	bake
варить	**16**	boil
запекать на функции "гриль"	**17**	broil
готовить на пару	**18**	steam
жарить	**19**	fry
пассеровать	**20**	saute
готовить на слабом огне	**21**	simmer
запекать	**22**	roast
готовить на гриле	**23**	barbecue / grill
обжарить помешивая	**24**	stir-fry
готовить в микроволновой печи	**25**	microwave

A. Can I help you?
B. Yes. Please **cut up** the vegetables.

[1–25]
A. What are you doing?
B. I'm _____ing the ....

[14–25]
A. How long should I _____ the ....?
B. _____ the .... for .... minutes/seconds.

What's your favorite recipe? Give instructions and use the units of measure on page 57. For example:

Mix a cup of flour and two tablespoons of sugar.
Add half a pound of butter.
Bake at 350° (degrees) for twenty minutes.

КУХОННАЯ УТВАРЬ

ложка для раздачи мороженого	1	ice cream scoop
открывалка	2	can opener
открывалка	3	bottle opener
овощечистка	4	(vegetable) peeler
взбиватель яиц	5	(egg) beater
крышка	6	lid/cover/top
кастрюля	7	pot
сковородка	8	frying pan/skillet
пароварка/кастрюля для приготовления пищи на водяной бане	9	double boiler
китайская сковородка	10	wok
половник	11	ladle
сито	12	strainer
лопатка	13	spatula
пароварка	14	steamer
нож	15	knife
чесночница	16	garlic press
терка	17	grater
блюдо для запеканок	18	casserole dish
жаровня	19	roasting pan
подставка в жаровне	20	roasting rack
нож для нарезки мяса	21	carving knife
ковшик	22	saucepan
дуршлаг	23	colander
кухонный таймер	24	kitchen timer
скалка	25	rolling pin
форма для выпечки	26	pie plate
нож для чистки овощей и фруктов	27	paring knife
противень	28	cookie sheet
формы для печенья	29	cookie cutter
миска	30	(mixing) bowl
венчик	31	whisk
мерный стаканчик	32	measuring cup
мерная ложка	33	measuring spoon
форма для торта	34	cake pan
деревянная ложка	35	wooden spoon

A. Could I possibly borrow your **ice cream scoop**?
B. Sure. I'll be happy to lend you my **ice cream scoop**.
A. Thanks.

A. What are you looking for?
B. I can't find the _____.
A. Look in that drawer/in that cabinet/on the counter/next to the _____/..............

[A Commercial]

Come to *Kitchen World*! We have everything you need for your kitchen, from _____s and _____s, to _____s and _____s. Are you looking for a new _____? Is it time to throw out your old _____? Come to *Kitchen World* today! We have everything you need!

What kitchen utensils and cookware do you have in your kitchen?

Which things do you use very often?

Which things do you rarely use?

гамбургер	**1** hamburger		замороженный йогурт	**15** frozen yogurt
чизбургер	**2** cheeseburger		молочный коктейль	**16** milkshake
хот дог	**3** hot dog		газированный напиток	**17** soda
сэндвич/бутерброд с рыбой	**4** fish sandwich		крышки	**18** lids
сэндвич/бутерброд с курицей	**5** chicken sandwich		бумажные стаканчики	**19** paper cups
жареная курица	**6** fried chicken		соломки	**20** straws
картофель фри	**7** french fries		салфетки	**21** napkins
кукурузные чипсы с соусом	**8** nachos		пластиковые приборы	**22** plastic utensils
такос	**9** taco		кетчуп	**23** ketchup
бурито	**10** burrito		горчица	**24** mustard
ломтик пиццы	**11** slice of pizza		майонез	**25** mayonnaise
тарелка "чили"	**12** bowl of chili		соус из маринованных огурцов	**26** relish
салат	**13** salad		заправка для салата	**27** salad dressing
мороженое	**14** ice cream			

A. May I help you?
B. Yes. I'd like a/an ___[1–5, 9–17]___ /
   an order of ___[6–8]___.

A. Excuse me. We're almost out of
   ___[18–27]___.
B. I'll get some more from the
   supply room. Thanks for telling
   me.

Do you go to fast-food restaurants? Which ones?
How often? What do you order?

Are there fast-food restaurants in your country?
Are they popular? What foods do they have?

пончик	**1**	donut	горячий шоколад	**20**	hot chocolate
кекс/маффин	**2**	muffin	молоко	**21**	milk
бублик	**3**	bagel	сэндвич с тунцом	**22**	tuna fish sandwich
сдобная булочка	**4**	bun	сэндвич с яичным салатом	**23**	egg salad sandwich
выпечка	**5**	danish/pastry	сэндвич с куриным салатом	**24**	chicken salad sandwich
несладкая выпечка	**6**	biscuit	сэндвич с ветчиной и сыром	**25**	ham and cheese sandwich
круассан	**7**	croissant	сэндвич с солониной	**26**	corned beef sandwich
яйцо	**8**	eggs	сэндвич с беконом, салатом и помидором	**27**	BLT/bacon, lettuce, and tomato sandwich
оладьи	**9**	pancakes	сэндвич с ростбифом	**28**	roast beef sandwich
вафли	**10**	waffles	белый хлеб	**29**	white bread
тост	**11**	toast	хлеб из цельной пшеницы	**30**	whole wheat bread
бекон	**12**	bacon	пита	**31**	pita bread
колбаски/сосиски	**13**	sausages	ржаной хлеб грубого помола	**32**	pumpernickel
жареный картофель	**14**	home fries	ржаной хлеб	**33**	rye bread
кофе	**15**	coffee	булочка	**34**	a roll
кофе без кофеина	**16**	decaf coffee	булочка	**35**	a submarine roll
чай	**17**	tea			
ледяной чай	**18**	iced tea			
лимонный напиток	**19**	lemonade			

A. May I help you?
B. Yes. I'd like a ____[1–7]____/an order of ____[8–14]____, please.
A. Anything to drink?
B. Yes. I'll have a small/medium-size/large/extra-large ____[15–21]____.

A. I'd like a ____[22–28]____ on ____[29–35]____, please.
B. What do you want on it?
A. Lettuce/tomato/mayonnaise/mustard/. . .

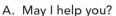

Do you like these foods? Which ones? Where do you get them? How often do you have them?

усаживать клиента (за стол)	**A**	seat the customers	детский стулt	**6** high chair
наливать воду	**B**	pour the water	подставка для сиденья	**7** booster seat
принимать заказ	**C**	take the order	меню	**8** menu
подавать еду	**D**	serve the meal	хлебница	**9** bread basket
сотрудница принимающая гостей/клиентов	**1**	hostess	сотрудник убирающий со столиков	**10** busperson
сотрудник принимающий гостей/клиентов	**2**	host	официантка/официант	**11** waitress/server
посетитель/клиент/клиент	**3**	diner/patron/customer	официант/официант	**12** waiter/server
мягкое сиденье-купе	**4**	booth	салат-бар	**13** salad bar
стол	**5**	table	зал ресторана	**14** dining room
			кухня	**15** kitchen
			шеф-повар	**16** chef

[4–9]
A. Would you like a **booth**?
B. Yes, please.

[10–12]
A. Hello. My name is *Julie*, and I'll be your **waitress** this evening.
B. Hello.

[1, 2, 13–16]
A. This restaurant has a wonderful **salad bar**.
B. I agree.

убирать со стола	**E**	clear the table		тарелка для супа	**26**	soup bowl
оплачивать счёт	**F**	pay the check		бокал для воды	**27**	water glass
оставлять чаевые	**G**	leave a tip		бокал для вина	**28**	wine glass
накрыть стол	**H**	set the table		чашка	**29**	cup
				блюдце	**30**	saucer
комната мытья посуды	**17**	dishroom		салфетка	**31**	napkin
мойщик посуды	**18**	dishwasher				
поднос	**19**	tray		**столовые приборы**	**silverware**	
тележка с десертами	**20**	dessert cart		вилка для салата	**32**	salad fork
счёт/чек	**21**	check		вилка для главного блюда	**33**	dinner fork
чаевые	**22**	tip		нож	**34**	knife
тарелка для салата	**23**	salad plate		чайная ложка	**35**	teaspoon
тарелка для хлеба и масла	**24**	bread-and-butter plate		ложка для супа	**36**	soup spoon
тарелка для главного блюда	**25**	dinner plate		нож для масла	**37**	butter knife

[A–H]
A. Please _____.
B. All right. I'll _____ right away.

[23–37]
A. Excuse me. Where does the _____ go?
B. It goes { to the left of the _____.
to the right of the _____.
on the _____.
between the _____ and the _____.

[1, 2, 10–12, 16, 18]
A. Do you have any job openings?
B. Yes. We're looking for a _____.

[23–37]
A. Excuse me. I dropped my _____.
B. That's okay. I'll get you another _____ from the kitchen.

Tell about a restaurant you know. Describe the place and the people. (Is the restaurant large or small? How many tables are there? How many people work there? Is there a salad bar? . . .)

МЕНЮ

фруктовый салат	**1** fruit cup/ fruit cocktail	блюдо с закусками	**10** antipasto (plate)
томатный сок	**2** tomato juice	салат "Цезарь"	**11** Caesar salad
закуска из креветок	**3** shrimp cocktail	рулет из фарша	**12** meatloaf
куриные крылышки	**4** chicken wings	ростбиф	**13** roast beef/ prime rib
кукурузные чипсы	**5** nachos	запечённая курица	**14** baked chicken
запечённые половинки картофеля	**6** potato skins	запечённая рыба	**15** broiled fish
		спагетти с фрикадельками	**16** spaghetti and meatballs
салат из овощей	**7** tossed salad/ garden salad	отбивная из телятины	**17** veal cutlet
салат "Греческий"	**8** Greek salad	запечённый картофель	**18** a baked potato
салат из шпината	**9** spinach salad	картофельное пюре	**19** mashed potatoes
		картофель фри	**20** french fries
		рис	**21** rice
		лапша	**22** noodles

овощная смесь	**23** mixed vegetables
шоколадный торт	**24** chocolate cake
яблочный пирог	**25** apple pie
мороженое	**26** ice cream
желе	**27** jello
пудинг	**28** pudding
десерт из мороженого	**29** ice cream sundae

[Ordering dinner]

A. May I take your order?
B. Yes, please. For the appetizer, I'd like the ____[1–6]____ .
A. And what kind of salad would you like?
B. I'll have the ____[7–11]____ .
A. And for the main course?
B. I'd like the ____[12–17]____ , please.
A. What side dish would you like with that?
B. Hmm. I think I'll have ____[18–23]____ .

[Ordering dessert]

A. Would you care for some dessert?
B. Yes. I'll have ____[24–28]____ /an ___[29]___ .

Tell about the food at a restaurant you know. What's on the menu?

What are some typical foods on the menus of restaurants in your country?

ЦВЕТА

красный	**1**	red	зелёный	**10**	green	
розовый	**2**	pink	светло-зелёный	**11**	light green	
оранжевый	**3**	orange	тёмно-зелёный	**12**	dark green	
жёлтый	**4**	yellow	фиолетовый	**13**	purple	
коричневый	**5**	brown	чёрный	**14**	black	
бежевый	**6**	beige	белый	**15**	white	
синий	**7**	blue	серый	**16**	gray	
тёмно-синий	**8**	navy blue	серебряный	**17**	silver	
бирюзовый	**9**	turquoise	золотой	**18**	gold	

A. What's your favorite color?
B. **Red**.

A. I like your _____ shirt.
You look very good in _____.

B. Thank you. _____ is my
favorite color.

A. My TV is broken.
B. What's the matter with it?
A. People's faces are _____,
the sky is _____, and the
grass is _____!

Do you know the flags of different countries?
What are the colors of flags you know?

What color makes you happy? What color
makes you sad? Why?

ОДЕЖДА

блузка	1	blouse	пиджак/жакет	11	sport coat/	детский сарафан	21	jumper
юбка	2	skirt			sport jacket/jacket	блейзер	22	blazer
рубашка	3	shirt	костюм	12	suit	туника	23	tunic
брюки	4	pants/slacks	костюм-тройка	13	three-piece suit	гамаши	24	leggings
рубашка	5	sport shirt	галстук	14	tie/necktie	комбинезон	25	overalls
джинсы	6	jeans	форма	15	uniform	водолазка	26	turtleneck
трикотажная	7	knit shirt/	футболка	16	T-shirt	смокинг	27	tuxedo
рубашка		jersey	шорты	17	shorts	бабочка	28	bow tie
платье	8	dress	платье для беременной	18	maternity dress	вечернее платье	29	(evening) gown
свитер	9	sweater	комбинезон	19	jumpsuit			
пиджак	10	jacket	жилет	20	vest			

A. I think I'll wear my new **blouse** today.
B. Good idea!

A. I really like your _____.
B. Thank you.
A. Where did you get it/them?
B. At ....

A. Oh, no! I just ripped my _____!
B. What a shame!

What clothing items in this lesson do you wear?
What color clothing do you like to wear?
What do you wear at work or at school? at parties? at weddings?

ВЕРХНЯЯ ОДЕЖДА

пальто	**1**	coat	ветровка	**11**	windbreaker	перчатки	**21**	gloves
пальто	**2**	overcoat	плащ-дождевик	**12**	raincoat	шапка-маска	**22**	ski mask
шляпа	**3**	hat	шляпа от дождя	**13**	rain hat	для лыжника		
куртка	**4**	jacket	плащ	**14**	trench coat	пуховик	**23**	down jacket
шарф	**5**	scarf/muffler	зонт	**15**	umbrella	варежки	**24**	mittens
вязаная куртка	**6**	sweater jacket	пончо	**16**	poncho	длинная куртка	**25**	parka
колготки	**7**	tights	куртка от дождя	**17**	rain jacket	с капюшоном		
кепка	**8**	cap	резиновые сапоги	**18**	rain boots	солнечные очки	**26**	sunglasses
кожаная куртка	**9**	leather jacket	шапка (вязаная)	**19**	ski hat	наушники от холода	**27**	ear muffs
бейсболка	**10**	baseball cap	куртка	**20**	ski jacket	жилет-пуховик	**28**	down vest

A. What's the weather like today?
B. It's cool/cold/raining/snowing.
A. I think I'll wear my _____.

[1–6, 8–17, 19, 20, 22, 23, 25, 28]
A. May I help you?
B. Yes, please. I'm looking for a/an _____.

[7, 18, 21, 24, 26, 27]
A. May I help you?
B. Yes, please. I'm looking for _____.

What do you wear outside when the weather is cool?/when it's raining?/when it's very cold?

SLEEPWEAR AND UNDERWEAR

НОЧНОЕ И НИЖНЕЕ БЕЛЬЁ

пижама	**1**	pajamas	мужские трусы	**9**	boxer shorts/boxers	майка	**16**	camisole
ночная рубашка	**2**	nightgown	бандаж	**10**	athletic supporter/ jockstrap	подъюбник	**17**	half slip
ночная рубашка	**3**	nightshirt	термобельё	**11**	long underwear/ long johns	комбинация	**18**	(full) slip
халат	**4**	bathrobe/robe				чулки	**19**	stockings
тапочки	**5**	slippers	носки	**12**	socks	колготки	**20**	pantyhose
спальный комбинезон	**6**	blanket sleeper	женские трусы	**13**	(bikini) panties	колготки	**21**	tights
футболка	**7**	undershirt/T-shirt	женские трусы	**14**	briefs/ underpants	гольфы	**22**	knee-highs
мужские трусы	**8**	(jockey) shorts/ underpants/briefs	бюстгальтер	**15**	bra	гольфы	**23**	knee socks

A. I can't find my new _____.
B. Did you look in the bureau/dresser/closet?
A. Yes, I did.
B. Then it's/they're probably in the wash.

What sleepwear items do you wear? What sleepwear items do people in your family wear?

СПОРТИВНАЯ ОДЕЖДА И ОБУВЬ

майка	**1**	tank top	купальник	**10**	swimsuit/ bathing suit	кроссовки	**19** running shoes
спортивные шорты	**2**	running shorts	плавки	**11**	swimming trunks/ swimsuit/ bathing suit	высокие кроссовки	**20** high-tops/ high-top sneakers
спортивная повязка на голову	**3**	sweatband	гимнастический купальник	**12**	leotard	босоножки/ сандалии	**21** sandals
спортивный костюм	**4**	jogging suit/ running suit/ warm-up suit	ботинки/туфли	**13**	shoes	шлёпанцы	**22** thongs/ flip-flops
футболка	**5**	T-shirt	туфли на каблуке	**14**	(high) heels	ботинки	**23** boots
велосипедные шорты	**6**	lycra shorts/ bike shorts	туфли-лодочки	**15**	pumps	рабочие ботинки	**24** work boots
толстовка	**7**	sweatshirt	мокасины	**16**	loafers	походные ботинки	**25** hiking boots
тренировочные брюки	**8**	sweatpants	кроссовки	**17**	sneakers/ athletic shoes	ковбойские сапоги	**26** cowboy boots
накидка	**9**	cover-up	теннисные туфли	**18**	tennis shoes	мокасины	**27** moccasins

[1–12]
A. Excuse me. I found this/these _____ in the dryer. Is it/Are they yours?
B. Yes. It's/They're mine. Thank you.

[13–27]
A. Are those new _____?
B. Yes, they are.
A. They're very nice.
B. Thanks.

Do you exercise? What do you do?
What kind of clothing do you wear when you exercise?

What kind of shoes do you wear when you go to work or to school?
when you exercise? when you relax at home?
when you go out with friends or family members?

ЮВЕЛИРНЫЕ УКРАШЕНИЯ И АКСЕССУАРЫ

кольцо	**1**	ring
кольцо для помолвки	**2**	engagement ring
обручальное кольцо	**3**	wedding ring/ wedding band
серёжки	**4**	earrings
цепочка	**5**	necklace
жемчужные бусы	**6**	pearl necklace/ pearls/ string of pearls
цепочка	**7**	chain
бусы	**8**	beads
брошь	**9**	pin/brooch
медальон	**10**	locket
браслет	**11**	bracelet
заколка	**12**	barrette
запонки	**13**	cuff links
подтяжки	**14**	suspenders
часы/ наручные часы	**15**	watch/ wrist watch
носовой платок	**16**	handkerchief
брелок	**17**	key ring/ key chain
кошелёк для мелочи	**18**	change purse
кошелёк	**19**	wallet
ремень	**20**	belt
дамская сумочка	**21**	purse/ handbag/ pocketbook
дамская сумочка	**22**	shoulder bag
сумка	**23**	tote bag
ранец/сумка для книг	**24**	book bag
рюкзак	**25**	backpack
косметичка	**26**	makeup bag
дипломат	**27**	briefcase

A. Oh, no! I think I lost my **ring**!
B. I'll help you look for it.

A. Oh, no! I think I lost my **earrings**!
B. I'll help you look for them.

[In a store]
A. Excuse me. Is this/Are these _____ on sale this week?
B. Yes. It's/They're half price.

[On the street]
A. Help! Police! Stop that man/woman!
B. What happened?!
A. He/She just stole my _____ and my _____!

Do you like to wear jewelry? What jewelry do you have?

In your country, what do men, women, and children use to carry their things?

ОПИСАНИЕ ОДЕЖДЫ

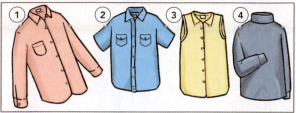

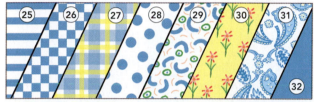

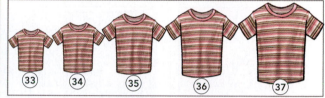

Виды Одежды		Types of Clothing
рубашка с длинным рукавом	**1**	long-sleeved shirt
рубашка с коротким рукавом	**2**	short-sleeved shirt
рубашка без рукавов	**3**	sleeveless shirt
водолазка	**4**	turtleneck (shirt)
свитер с треугольным вырезом	**5**	V-neck sweater
кофта	**6**	cardigan sweater
свитер	**7**	crewneck sweater
свитер "с горлышком"	**8**	turtleneck sweater
гольфы	**9**	knee-high socks
носки	**10**	ankle socks
носки	**11**	crew socks
серёжки	**12**	pierced earrings
клипсы	**13**	clip-on earrings

Виды Ткани		Types of Material
вельветовые *брюки*	**14**	corduroy *pants*
кожаные *сапоги*	**15**	leather *boots*
нейлоновые *чулки*	**16**	nylon *stockings*
хлопчатобумажная *футболка*	**17**	cotton *T-shirt*
джинсовый *жакет*	**18**	denim *jacket*

фланелевая *рубашка*	**19**	flannel *shirt*
блузка из полиэстера	**20**	polyester *blouse*
льняное *платье*	**21**	linen *dress*
шёлковый *шарф*	**22**	silk *scarf*
шерстяной *свитер*	**23**	wool *sweater*
соломенная *шляпа*	**24**	straw *hat*

Текстильный Рисунок		Patterns
полосатый	**25**	striped
клетчатый	**26**	checked
шотландка	**27**	plaid
в горошек	**28**	polka-dotted
узорчатый	**29**	patterned/print
с цветочным рисунком	**30**	flowered/floral
с рисунком пейсли	**31**	paisley
однотонный *синий*	**32**	solid *blue*

Размеры		Sizes
размер 42-44	**33**	extra-small
размер 44-46	**34**	small
размер 46-48	**35**	medium
размер 48-50	**36**	large
размер 50-52	**37**	extra-large

[1–24]
A. May I help you?
B. Yes, please. I'm looking for a *shirt*.*
A. What kind?
B. I'm looking for a *long-sleeved shirt*.

* *With 9–16:* I'm looking for _____.

[25–32]
A. How do you like this _____ tie/shirt/skirt?
B. Actually, I prefer that _____ one.

[33–37]
A. What size are you looking for?
B. _____.

Describe your favorite clothing items. For each item, tell about the color, the type of material, the size, and the pattern.

ДЕФЕКТЫ ОДЕЖДЫ И ИХ УСТРАНЕНИЕ

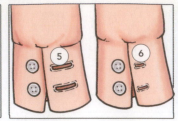
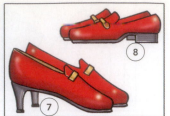

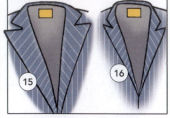

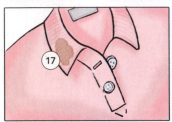
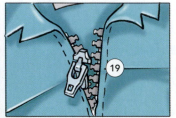

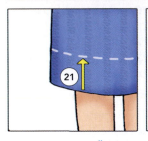

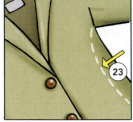

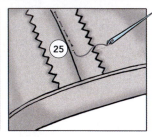

длинный – короткий	**1–2** long – short	пятно на *воротнике*	**17** stained *collar*
обтягивающий – широкий/ свободный	**3–4** tight – loose/ baggy	оборванный *карман*	**18** ripped/torn *pocket*
большой – маленький	**5–6** large/big – small	сломанная *молния*	**19** broken *zipper*
высокий – низкий	**7–8** high – low	оторванная *пуговица*	**20** missing *button*
необычный – простой	**9–10** fancy – plain	подшивать *юбку*	**21** shorten the *skirt*
тяжёлый – лёгкий	**11–12** heavy – light	удлинять *рукава*	**22** lengthen the *sleeves*
тёмный – светлый	**13–14** dark – light	ушивать *пиджак*	**23** take in the *jacket*
широкий – узкий	**15–16** wide – narrow	выпускать *брюки*	**24** let out the *pants*
		ремонтировать *шов*	**25** fix/repair the *seam*

[1–2]
A. Are the sleeves too **long**?
B. No. They're too **short**.

1–2 Are the sleeves too _____?
3–4 Are the pants too _____?
5–6 Are the buttonholes too _____?
7–8 Are the heels too _____?

9–10 Are the buttons too _____?
11–12 Is the coat too _____?
13–14 Is the color too _____?
15–16 Are the lapels too _____?

[17–20]
A. What's the matter with it?
B. It has a **stained** *collar*.

[21–25]
A. Please **shorten** the *skirt*.
B. **Shorten** the *skirt*? Okay.

Tell about the differences between clothing people wear now and clothing people wore a long time ago.

СТИРКА

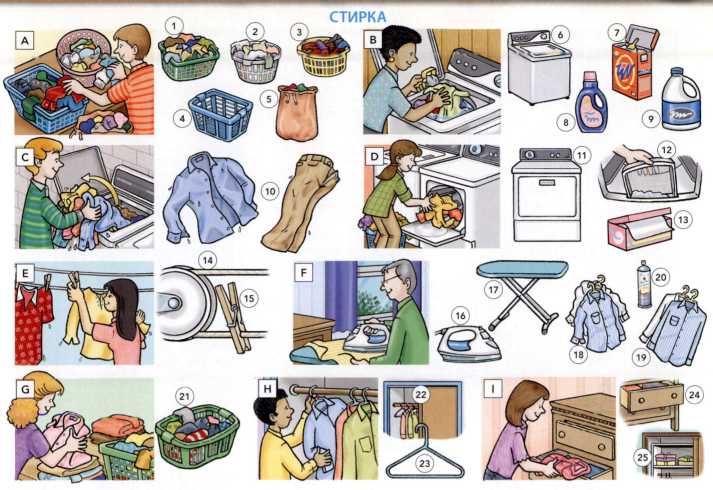

сортировать стирку	**A**	sort the laundry
загрузить стиральную машину	**B**	load the washer
разгрузить стиральную машину	**C**	unload the washer
загрузить сушку	**D**	load the dryer
развешивать одежду на бельевую верёвку	**E**	hang clothes on the clothesline
гладить	**F**	iron
складывать чистую одежду	**G**	fold the laundry
повесить одежду на плечики	**H**	hang up clothing
сложить вещи по местам	**I**	put things away

стирка	**1**	laundry
светлая одежда	**2**	light clothing
тёмная одежда	**3**	dark clothing
корзина для стирки	**4**	laundry basket
мешок для стирки	**5**	laundry bag
стиральная машина	**6**	washer/washing machine
стиральный порошок	**7**	laundry detergent
кондиционер для белья	**8**	fabric softener

отбеливатель	**9**	bleach
мокрая одежда	**10**	wet clothing
сушка/сушильная машина	**11**	dryer
фильтр в сушке	**12**	lint trap
антистатик	**13**	static cling remover
бельевая верёвка	**14**	clothesline
прищепка	**15**	clothespin
утюг	**16**	iron
гладильная доска	**17**	ironing board
мятая одежда	**18**	wrinkled clothing
глаженная одежда	**19**	ironed clothing
спрэй для накрахмаливания одежды	**20**	spray starch
чистая одежда	**21**	clean clothing
ниша	**22**	closet
вешалка/плечики	**23**	hanger
отделение/ящик	**24**	drawer
полка-полки	**25**	shelf-shelves

[A–I]
A. What are you doing?
B. I'm _____ing.

[4–6, 11, 14–17, 23]
A. Excuse me. Do you sell _____s?
B. Yes. They're at the back of the store.
A. Thank you.

[7–9, 13, 20]
A. Excuse me. Do you sell _____?
B. Yes. It's at the back of the store.
A. Thank you.

Who does the laundry in your home? What things does this person use?

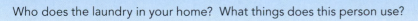

УНИВЕРМАГ

план магазина	**1**	(store) directory	
Прилавок Ювелирного Отдела	**2**	Jewelry Counter	
Прилавок Парфюмерного Отдела	**3**	Perfume Counter	
эскалатор	**4**	escalator	
лифт	**5**	elevator	
Отдел Мужской Одежды	**6**	Men's Clothing Department	
выдача товара	**7**	customer pickup area	
Отдел Женской Одежды	**8**	Women's Clothing Department	
Отдел Детской Одежды	**9**	Children's Clothing Department	
Отдел Предметов Домашнего Обихода	**10**	Housewares Department	
Отдел Мебели	**11**	Furniture Department/ Home Furnishings Department	
Отдел Бытовой Техники	**12**	Household Appliances Department	
Отдел Электроники	**13**	Electronics Department	
Информация	**14**	Customer Assistance Counter/ Customer Service Counter	
мужской туалет	**15**	men's room	
женский туалет	**16**	ladies' room	
фонтан с питьевой водой	**17**	water fountain	
закусочная	**18**	snack bar	
Отдел Упаковки Подарков	**19**	Gift Wrap Counter	

A. Excuse me. Where's the **store directory**?
B. It's over there, next to the **Jewelry Counter**.
A. Thanks.
B. You're welcome.

A. Excuse me. Do you sell *ties**?
B. Yes. You can find *ties** in the ___[6, 8–13]___ /at the ___[2, 3]___ on the first/second/third/fourth floor.
A. Thank you.

**ties/bracelets/dresses/toasters/. . .*

Describe a department store you know. Tell what is on each floor.

ПОКУПКИ

покупать	**A** buy	вывеска "распродажа"	**1** sale sign	руководство по уходу	**8** care instructions
возвращать	**B** return	ярлык/этикетка	**2** label	обычная цена	**9** regular price
обменивать	**C** exchange	ценник	**3** price tag	цена со скидкой	**10** sale price
примерять	**D** try on	чек	**4** receipt	цена	**11** price
оплачивать	**E** pay for	скидка	**5** discount	налог с продаж	**12** sales tax
узнавать о (товаре)	**F** get some information about	размер	**6** size	итоговая цена	**13** total price
		состав ткани	**7** material		

A. May I help you?
B. Yes, please. I want to _____[A–F]_____ this item.
A. Certainly. I'll be glad to help you.

A. { What's the _____[5–7, 9–13]_____?
   { What are the _____[8]_____?
B. _____.
A. Are you sure?
B. Yes. Look at the _____[1–4]_____!

Which stores in your area have sales? How often?

Tell about something you bought on sale.

ВИДЕО И АУДИО ТЕХНИКА

телевизор	1	TV/television
плазменный телевизор	2	plasma TV
ЖК телевизор	3	LCD TV
проекционный телевизор	4	projection TV
переносной/портативный телевизор	5	portable TV
пульт (дистанционного управления)	6	remote (control)
DVD (диск)	7	DVD
DVD проигрыватель/плеер	8	DVD player
видеокассета	9	video/videocassette/videotape
видеомагнитофон	10	VCR/videocassette recorder
видеокамера	11	camcorder/video camera
аккумуляторные батарейки	12	battery pack
зарядное устройство	13	battery charger
радио	14	radio
радио-часы	15	clock radio
транзистор	16	shortwave radio
магнитофон	17	tape recorder/cassette recorder
микрофон	18	microphone

музыкальный центр	19	stereo system/sound system
пластинка	20	record
проигрыватель	21	turntable
CD/ компакт диск	22	CD/compact disc
CD проигрыватель	23	CD player
радиоприёмное устройство	24	tuner
аудио кассета/кассета	25	(audio)tape/(audio)cassette
кассетный проигрыватель	26	tape deck/cassette deck
динамики	27	speakers
портативный магнитофон	28	portable stereo system/boombox
CD плеер	29	portable/personal CD player
аудио плеер	30	portable/personal cassette player
наушники	31	headphones
MP3 плеер	32	portable/personal digital audio player
игровая приставка	33	video game system
видео игра	34	video game
портативная игровая система	35	hand-held video game

A. May I help you?
B. Yes, please. I'm looking for a **TV**.

* With 27 & 31, use: I'm looking for _____.

A. I like your new _____.
   Where did you get it/them?
B. At ..... (name of store) ....

A. Which company makes the best _____?
B. In my opinion, the best _____ is/are made by ....

What video and audio equipment do you have or want?

In your opinion, which brands of video and audio equipment are the best?

ТЕЛЕФОНЫ И ФОТОПРИБОРЫ

телефон	**1**	telephone/phone		
радио телефон	**2**	cordless phone		
мобильный телефон	**3**	cell phone/cellular phone		
батарейка	**4**	battery		
зарядное устройство	**5**	battery charger		
автоответчик	**6**	answering machine		
пейджер	**7**	pager		
КПК/карманный компьютер	**8**	PDA/electronic personal organizer		
факс	**9**	fax machine		
карманный калькулятор	**10**	(pocket) calculator		
счётная машинка	**11**	adding machine		
регулятор напряжения	**12**	voltage regulator		

адаптер	**13**	adapter
фотоаппарат	**14**	(35 millimeter) camera
линза	**15**	lens
фотоплёнка	**16**	film
трансфокатор	**17**	zoom lens
цифровой фотоаппарат	**18**	digital camera
карта памяти	**19**	memory disk
штатив	**20**	tripod
вспышка	**21**	flash (attachment)
футляр для фотоаппарата	**22**	camera case
диапроектор	**23**	slide projector
экран	**24**	(movie) screen

A. Can I help you?
B. Yes. I want to buy a **telephone**.*

* With 16, use: I want to buy _____.

A. Excuse me. Do you sell _____s?*
B. Yes. We have a large selection of _____s.

* With 16, use the singular.

A. Which _____ is the best?
B. This one here. It's made by _____.
(*company*)

What kind of telephone do you use?

Do you have a camera? What kind is it?
What do you take pictures of?

Does anyone you know have an answering machine?
When you call, what message do you hear?

КОМПЬЮТЕРЫ

Аппаратное Обеспечение Компьютера		Computer Hardware
настольный ПК	**1**	(desktop) computer
центральный процессор	**2**	CPU/central processing unit
монитор	**3**	monitor/screen
дисковод для компакт дисков	**4**	CD-ROM drive
компьютерный компакт-диск	**5**	CD-ROM
дисковод	**6**	disk drive
дискета	**7**	(floppy) disk
клавиатура	**8**	keyboard
мышь	**9**	mouse
ЖК монитор	**10**	flat panel screen/ LCD screen
ноутбук	**11**	notebook computer

ручка управления/джойстик	**12**	joystick
шаровой манипулятор	**13**	track ball
модем	**14**	modem
ограничитель перенапряжения	**15**	surge protector
принтер	**16**	printer
сканер	**17**	scanner
кабель	**18**	cable

Программное Обеспечение Компьютера		Computer Software
текстовый процессор	**19**	word-processing program
табличный процессор	**20**	spreadsheet program
образовательная компьютерная программа	**21**	educational software program
компьютерная игра	**22**	computer game

A. Can you recommend a good **computer**?
B. Yes. This **computer** here is excellent.

A. Is that a new _____?
B. Yes.
A. Where did you get it?
B. At ....(name of store)..............

A. May I help you?
B. Yes, please. Do you sell _____s?
A. Yes. We carry a complete line of _____s.

Do you use a computer? When?

In your opinion, how have computers changed the world?

МАГАЗИН ИГРУШЕК

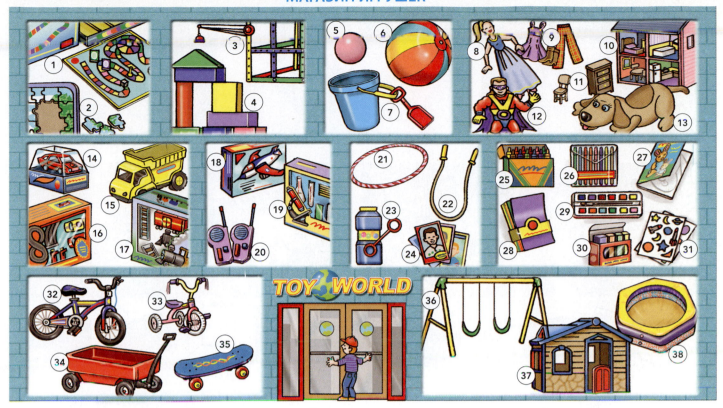

настольная игра	**1**	board game
настольная игра-мозаика	**2**	(jigsaw) puzzle
конструктор	**3**	construction set
кубики	**4**	(building) blocks
резиновый мяч	**5**	rubber ball
надувной мяч	**6**	beach ball
ведёрко и совок	**7**	pail and shovel
кукла	**8**	doll
одежда для куклы	**9**	doll clothing
кукольный домик	**10**	doll house
кукольная мебель	**11**	doll house furniture
кукла для мальчиков	**12**	action figure
мягкая игрушка	**13**	stuffed animal
модельная игрушечная машина	**14**	matchbox car
игрушечный грузовик	**15**	toy truck
набор гоночных машин	**16**	racing car set
железная дорога	**17**	train set
набор для сбора модели	**18**	model kit
набор "учёного"	**19**	science kit

детская рация	**20**	walkie-talkie (set)
обруч	**21**	hula hoop
скакалка	**22**	jump rope
мыльные пузыри	**23**	bubble soap
коллекционные карточки	**24**	trading cards
восковые карандаши	**25**	crayons
фломастеры	**26**	(color) markers
книжка-раскраска	**27**	coloring book
набор цветной бумаги	**28**	construction paper
краски	**29**	paint set
пластилин	**30**	(modeling) clay
наклейки	**31**	stickers
велосипед	**32**	bicycle
трёхколёсный велосипед	**33**	tricycle
тележка	**34**	wagon
скейтборд	**35**	skateboard
качели	**36**	swing set
игрушечный домик	**37**	play house
надувной бассейн/ детский бассейн	**38**	kiddie pool/ inflatable pool

A. Excuse me. I'm looking for (a/an) _____(s) for my *grandson*.*
B. Look in the next aisle.
A. Thank you.

* *grandson/granddaughter/. . .*

A. I don't know what to get my ....-year-old son/daughter for his/her birthday.
B. What about (a) _____?
A. Good idea! Thanks.

A. Mom/Dad? Can we buy this/these _____?
B. No, *Johnny*. Not today.

What toys are most popular in your country?

What were your favorite toys when you were a child?

БАНК

ставить деньги на счёт	**A** make a deposit	сертифицированный банковский чек для путешествий	**4** traveler's check
снимать деньги со счёта	**B** make a withdrawal	банковская расчётная книжка	**5** bankbook/passbook
обналичваить чек	**C** cash a check	банковская карта	**6** ATM card
покупать сертифицированные банковские чеки для путешествий	**D** get traveler's checks	кредитная карта	**7** credit card
открывать счёт	**E** open an account	банковский сейф	**8** (bank) vault
заполнять анкету на долг	**F** apply for a loan	личный ящик в сейфе	**9** safe deposit box
обменивать валюту	**G** exchange currency	банковский кассир	**10** teller
		охранник	**11** security guard
квитанция на вклад	**1** deposit slip	банкомат	**12** ATM (machine)/ cash machine
квитанция на получение/снятие денег	**2** withdrawal slip	сотрудник банка	**13** bank officer
чек	**3** check		

[A–G]
A. Where are you going?
B. I'm going to the bank.
   I have to _____.

[5–7]
A. What are you looking for?
B. My _____. I can't find it anywhere!

[8–13]
A. How many _____s does the State Street Bank have?
B. ....

Do you have a bank account? What kind? Where? What do you do at the bank?

Do you ever use traveler's checks? When?

Do you have a credit card? What kind? When do you use it?

ФИНАНСЫ

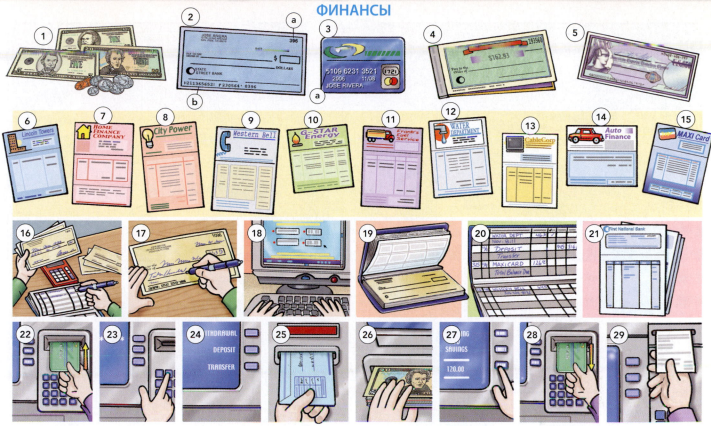

Виды Оплаты — Forms of Payment

Русский	№	English
наличные	1	cash
чек	2	check
номер чека	a	check number
номер счёта	b	account number
кредитная карта	3	credit card
номер кредитной карты	a	credit card number
сертифицированный банковский чек	4	money order
сертифицированный банковский чек для путешествий	5	traveler's check

Счета за Бытовые Услуги — Household Bills

Русский	№	English
аренда	6	rent
оплата кредита на недвижимость	7	mortgage payment
счёт за электричество	8	electric bill
счёт за телефон	9	telephone bill
счёт за газ	10	gas bill
счёт за отопление	11	oil bill/heating bill
счёт за воду	12	water bill
счёт за кабельное телевидение	13	cable TV bill
оплата кредита за машину	14	car payment
счёт на кредитную карту	15	credit card bill

Семейные Финансы — Family Finances

Русский	№	English
подводить баланс в чековой книжке	16	balance the checkbook
выписывать чек	17	write a check
электронный банкинг	18	bank online
чековая книжка	19	checkbook
книжка учёта чеков/чековый регистр	20	check register
ежемесячный отчёт по банковскому счёту	21	monthly statement

Использование Банкомата — Using an ATM Machine

Русский	№	English
вставьте банковскую карту	22	insert the ATM card
введите свой ПИН-код/введите свой личный код счёта	23	enter your PIN number/personal identification number
выберите операцию	24	select a transaction
ставить деньги на счёт	25	make a deposit
снимать наличные	26	withdraw/get cash
перевести деньги	27	transfer funds
достаньте карту	28	remove your card
получите чек	29	take your transaction slip/receipt

A. Can I pay by ___[1, 2]___/ with a ___[3–5]___?
B. Yes. We accept ___[1]___/ ___[2–5]___s.

A. What are you doing?
B. I'm paying the ___[6–15]___.
   I'm ___[16–18]___ing.
   I'm looking for the ___[19–21]___.

A. What should I do?
B. ___[22–29]___.

What household bills do you receive?
How much do you pay for the different bills?

Who takes care of the finances in your household? What does that person do?

Do you use ATM machines?
If you do, how do you use them?

ПОЧТА

письмо	**1**	letter	анкета на воинскую повинность	**16** selective service registration form
открытка	**2**	postcard	анкета на получение паспорта	**17** passport application form
авиаписьмо/ аэрограмма	**3**	air letter/ aerogramme	конверт	**18** envelope
посылка/бандероль	**4**	package/parcel	адрес отправителя	**19** return address
первый класс	**5**	first class	адрес получателя	**20** mailing address
ускоренная почта	**6**	priority mail	индекс	**21** zip code
экспресс почта	**7**	express mail/ overnight mail	штемпель	**22** postmark
мелкий пакет/бандероль	**8**	parcel post	марка	**23** stamp/postage
сертифицированная почта	**9**	certified mail	почтовая ячейка	**24** mail slot
марка	**10**	stamp	сотрудник почты	**25** postal worker/postal clerk
комплект марок	**11**	sheet of stamps	весы	**26** scale
комплект марок	**12**	roll of stamps	автомат продажи марок	**27** stamp machine
комплект марок	**13**	book of stamps	почтальон	**28** letter carrier/mail carrier
сертифицированный почтой чек	**14**	money order	почтовая машина	**29** mail truck
анкета о смене адреса	**15**	change-of-address form	почтовый ящик	**30** mailbox

[1–4]
A. Where are you going?
B. To the post office. I have to mail a/an _____ .

[5–9]
A. How do you want to send it?
B. _____ , please.

[10–17]
A. Next!
B. I'd like a _____ , please.
A. Here you are.

[19–21, 23]
A. Do you want me to mail this letter?
B. Yes, thanks.
A. Oops! You forgot the _____ !

How often do you go to the post office? What do you do there?   Tell about the postal system in your country.

БИБЛИОТЕКА

Russian	#	English
интернет каталог	1	online catalog
картотека	2	card catalog
автор	3	author
название книги	4	title
библиотечная карточка	5	library card
копировальная машина	6	copier/photocopier/copy machine
полки	7	shelves
детский отдел	8	children's section
детская книга	9	children's books
отдел периодики	10	periodical section
академические журналы	11	journals
журналы	12	magazines
газеты	13	newspapers
отдел звукозаписи	14	media section
книги на кассете	15	books on tape
аудиокассеты	16	audiotapes
CD диски	17	CDs
видеокассеты	18	videotapes
программное обеспечение	19	(computer) software
DVD диски	20	DVDs
отдел иностранных языков	21	foreign language section
книги на иностранных языках	22	foreign language books
отдел-справочная	23	reference section
микрофильм	24	microfilm
читальный аппарат для микрофильмов	25	microfilm reader
словарь	26	dictionary
энциклопедия	27	encyclopedia
атлас	28	atlas
стол справок	29	reference desk
библиотекарь	30	(reference) librarian
стол выдачи и регистрации книг	31	checkout desk
сотрудник библиотеки	32	library clerk

[1, 2, 6–32]
A. Excuse me. Where's/Where are the _____?
B. Over there, at/near/next to the _____.

[8–23, 26–28]
A. Excuse me. Where can I find a/an ___[26–28]___ / ___[9, 11–13, 15–20, 22]___?
B. Look in the ___[8, 10, 14, 21, 23]___ over there.

A. I'm having trouble finding a book.
B. Do you know the ___[3–4]___?
A. Yes. ....

A. Excuse me. I'd like to check out this ___[26–28]___/these ___[11–13]___.
B. I'm sorry. It/They must remain in the library.

Do you go to a library? Where? What does this library have?

Tell about how you use the library.

РАЙОННЫЕ УЧРЕЖДЕНИЯ

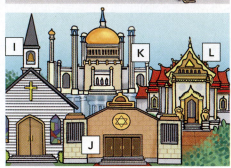

полицейский участок	**A**	police station	пожарник	**5** firefighter
пожарная станция	**B**	fire station	комната скорой помощи	**6** emergency room
больница	**C**	hospital	сотрудник скорой помощи/ медработник	**7** EMT/paramedic
здание мэрии	**D**	town hall/city hall	машина скорой помощи	**8** ambulance
дом культуры/центр отдыха	**E**	recreation center	мэр города	**9** mayor/city manager
свалка	**F**	dump	приёмная	**10** meeting room
детский сад	**G**	child-care center	спортзал	**11** gym
дом престарелых	**H**	senior center	организатор досуга	**12** activities director
церковь	**I**	church	комната игр	**13** game room
синагога	**J**	synagogue	бассейн	**14** swimming pool
мечеть	**K**	mosque	мусорщик	**15** sanitation worker
храм	**L**	temple	центр переработки отходов	**16** recycling center
оператор службы спасения	**1**	emergency operator	сотрудник детского сада	**17** child-care worker
полицейский	**2**	police officer	детская комната	**18** nursery
полицейская машина	**3**	police car	игровая комната	**19** playroom
пожарная машина	**4**	fire engine	сотрудник дома престарелых	**20** eldercare worker/ senior care worker

[A–L]
A. Where are you going?
B. I'm going to the _____.

[1, 2, 5, 7, 12, 15, 17, 20]
A. What do you do?
B. I'm a/an _____.

[3, 4, 8]
A. Do you hear a siren?
B. Yes. There's a/an _____ coming up behind us.

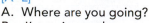

What community institutions are in your city or town? Where are they located?

Which community institutions do you use? When?

ПРЕСТУПЛЕНИЯ И ЭКСТРЕННЫЕ СЛУЧАИ

автоавария	**1**	car accident
пожар	**2**	fire
взрыв	**3**	explosion
ограбление	**4**	robbery
воровство	**5**	burglary
ограбление	**6**	mugging
похищение людей	**7**	kidnapping
потерянный ребёнок	**8**	lost child
угон машины	**9**	car jacking
ограбление банка	**10**	bank robbery
нападение	**11**	assault
убийство	**12**	murder

авария энергосистемы/ прекращение подачи электроэнергии	**13**	blackout/ power outage
утечка газа	**14**	gas leak
неисправность водопровода	**15**	water main break
неисправность линии высокого напряжения	**16**	downed power line
химический сброс	**17**	chemical spill
крушение поезда	**18**	train derailment
вандализм/варварство	**19**	vandalism
гангстерское насилие	**20**	gang violence
вождение в пьяном виде	**21**	drunk driving
наркоторговля	**22**	drug dealing

[1–13]
A. I want to report a/an _____.
B. What's your location?
A. ....

[14–18]
A. Why is this street closed?
B. It's closed because of a _____.

[19–22]
A. I'm very concerned about the amount of _____ in our community.
B. I agree. _____ is a very serious problem.

Is there much crime in your community? Tell about it.

Have you ever experienced a crime or emergency? What happened?

ЧАСТИ ТЕЛА

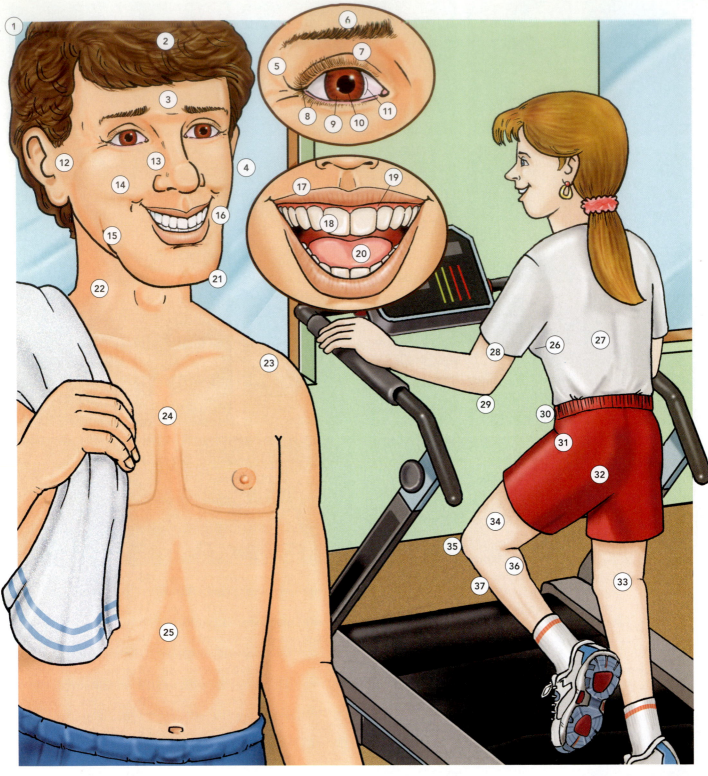

голова	**1**	head	зрачок	**10**	pupil
волосы	**2**	hair	роговица	**11**	cornea
лоб	**3**	forehead	ухо	**12**	ear
лицо	**4**	face	нос	**13**	nose
глаз	**5**	eye	щека	**14**	cheek
бровь	**6**	eyebrow	челюсть	**15**	jaw
веко	**7**	eyelid	рот	**16**	mouth
ресницы	**8**	eyelashes	губа	**17**	lip
радужная	**9**	iris	зуб-зубы	**18**	tooth–teeth
оболочка			дёсны	**19**	gums

язык	**20**	tongue	талия	**30**	waist
подбородок	**21**	chin	бедро	**31**	hip
шея	**22**	neck	ягодицы	**32**	buttocks
плечо	**23**	shoulder	нога	**33**	leg
грудь	**24**	chest	бедро	**34**	thigh
живот	**25**	abdomen	колено	**35**	knee
грудь/бюст	**26**	breast	икра	**36**	calf
спина	**27**	back	голень	**37**	shin
рука	**28**	arm			
локоть	**29**	elbow			

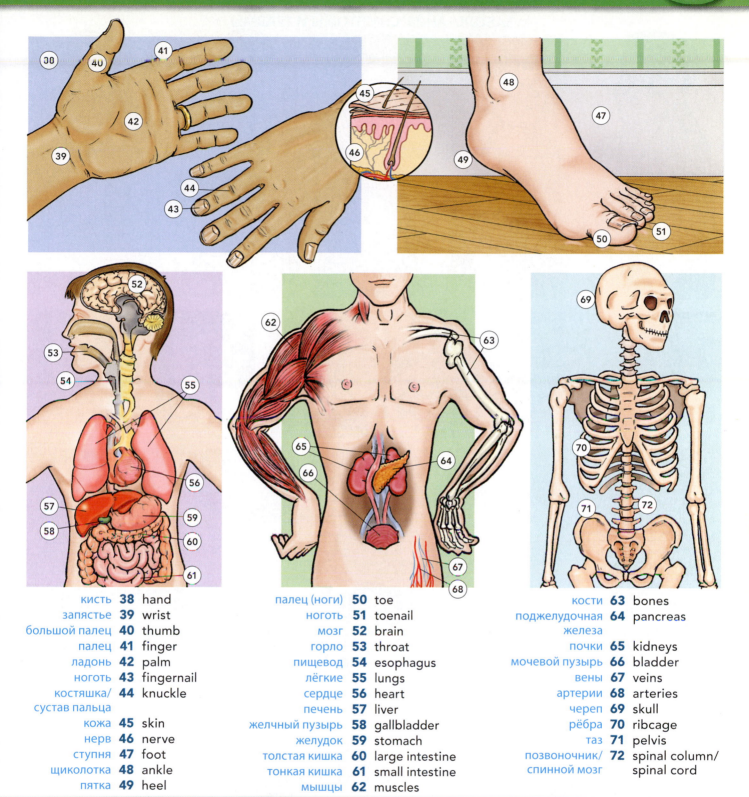

кисть	38	hand
запястье	39	wrist
большой палец	40	thumb
палец	41	finger
ладонь	42	palm
ноготь	43	fingernail
костяшка/	44	knuckle
сустав пальца		
кожа	45	skin
нерв	46	nerve
ступня	47	foot
щиколотка	48	ankle
пятка	49	heel

палец (ноги)	50	toe
ноготь	51	toenail
мозг	52	brain
горло	53	throat
пищевод	54	esophagus
лёгкие	55	lungs
сердце	56	heart
печень	57	liver
желчный пузырь	58	gallbladder
желудок	59	stomach
толстая кишка	60	large intestine
тонкая кишка	61	small intestine
мышцы	62	muscles

кости	63	bones
поджелудочная	64	pancreas
железа		
почки	65	kidneys
мочевой пузырь	66	bladder
вены	67	veins
артерии	68	arteries
череп	69	skull
рёбра	70	ribcage
таз	71	pelvis
позвоночник/	72	spinal column/
спинной мозг		spinal cord

A. My doctor checked my **head** and said everything is okay.
B. I'm glad to hear that.

[1, 3–7, 12–29, 31–51]

A. Ooh!
B. What's the matter?
{ My _____ hurts!
{ My _____s hurt!

[52–72]

A. My doctor wants me to have some tests.
B. Why?
A. She's concerned about my _____.

Describe yourself as completely as you can.

Which parts of the body are most important at school? at work? when you play your favorite sport?

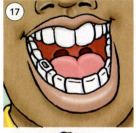

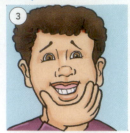

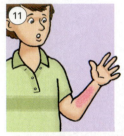

головная боль	**1**	headache
боль в ухе	**2**	earache
зубная боль	**3**	toothache
боль в животе	**4**	stomachache
боль в спине	**5**	backache
фарингит	**6**	sore throat
температура	**7**	fever/temperature
простуда	**8**	cold
кашель	**9**	cough
инфекция	**10**	infection

сыпь	**11**	rash
укус насекомого	**12**	insect bite
солнечный ожог	**13**	sunburn
кривошея	**14**	stiff neck
насморк	**15**	runny nose
носовое кровотечение	**16**	bloody nose
кариес	**17**	cavity
мозоль	**18**	blister
бородавка	**19**	wart

икание	**20**	(the) hiccups
озноб	**21**	(the) chills
колики/приступ острой боли	**22**	cramps
понос	**23**	diarrhea
боль в груди	**24**	chest pain
одышка	**25**	shortness of breath
ларингит	**26**	laryngitis

A. What's the matter?
B. I have a/an [1–19].

A. What's the matter?
B. I have [20–26].

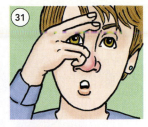

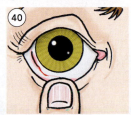

обморок	**27**	faint	хрипеть	**35**	wheeze	ожог	**43**	burn
головокружение	**28**	dizzy	рыгать	**36**	burp	повредить–повредил	**44**	hurt–hurt
тошнота	**29**	nauseous	рвать	**37**	vomit/throw up	поранить–поранил	**45**	cut–cut
вздутие	**30**	bloated	кровоточить	**38**	bleed	растянуть	**46**	sprain
заложенный	**31**	congested	подворачивать	**39**	twist	вывихнуть	**47**	dislocate
обессиленный	**32**	exhausted	царапина	**40**	scratch	сломать–сломал	**48**	break–broke
кашлять	**33**	cough	царапина	**41**	scrape	отёкший	**49**	swollen
чихать	**34**	sneeze	синяк	**42**	bruise	зудящий	**50**	itchy

A. What's the problem?

B. { I feel [27–30] .
I'm [31–32] .
I've been [33–38] ing a lot. }

A. What happened?

B. { I [39–45] ed my ....
I think I [46–48] ed my ....
My .... is/are [49–50] . }

A. How do you feel?

B. Not so good. / Not very well. / Terrible!

A. What's the matter?

B. .... , ... , and ....

A. I'm sorry to hear that.

Tell about the last time you didn't feel well. What was the matter?

Tell about a time you hurt yourself. What happened? How? What did you do about it?

What do you do when you have a cold? a stomachache? an insect bite? the hiccups?

ПЕРВАЯ ПОМОЩЬ

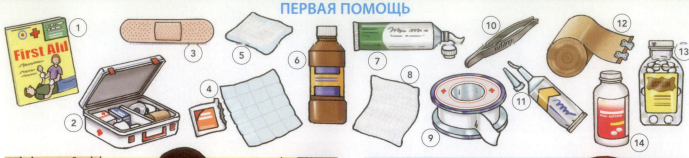

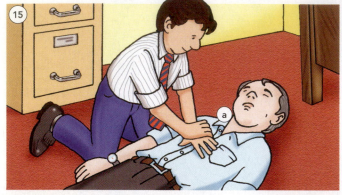

инструкции по оказанию первой помощи	**1** first-aid manual
аптечка	**2** first-aid kit
пластырь	**3** (adhesive) bandage/ Band-Aid™
салфетка антисептическая	**4** antiseptic cleansing wipe
стерильная салфетка	**5** sterile (dressing) pad
перекись водорода	**6** hydrogen peroxide
мазь с антибиотиком	**7** antibiotic ointment
марля	**8** gauze
лейкопластырь	**9** adhesive tape
пинцет	**10** tweezers
противоаллергическая мазь	**11** antihistamine cream
эластичный бинт/бинт	**12** elastic bandage/ Ace™ bandage

аспирин	**13** aspirin
обезболивающее средство	**14** non-aspirin pain reliever
сердечно-лёгочная реанимация	**15** CPR (cardiopulmonary resuscitation)
отсутствие пульса	**a** has no pulse
искусственное дыхание	**16** rescue breathing
не дышит	**b** isn't breathing
приём Хеймлиха	**17** the Heimlich maneuver
подавиться	**c** is choking
шина	**18** splint
сломал палец	**d** broke a finger
жгут	**19** tourniquet
кровоточит	**e** is bleeding

A. Do we have any ___[3–5, 12]___s/ ___[6–11, 13, 14]___ ?
B. Yes. Look in the first-aid kit.

A. Help! My friend ___[a–e]___ !
B. I can help!
  I know how to do ___[15–17]___.
  I can make a ___[18, 19]___.

Do you have a first-aid kit? If you do, what's in it? If you don't, where can you buy one?

Tell about a time when you gave or received first aid.

Where can a person learn first aid in your community?

ЭКСТРЕННЫЕ МЕДИЦИНСКИЕ СЛУЧАИ И БОЛЕЗНИ

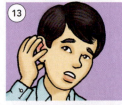

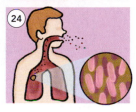
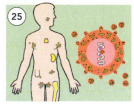

ушиб/травмированный	**1** hurt/injured		ангина	**14** strep throat
в шоковом состоянии	**2** in shock		корь	**15** measles
без сознания	**3** unconscious		свинка	**16** mumps
тепловой удар	**4** heatstroke		ветрянка/ветряная оспа	**17** chicken pox
обморожение	**5** frostbite		астма	**18** asthma
сердечный приступ	**6** heart attack		рак	**19** cancer
аллергическая реакция	**7** allergic reaction		депрессия	**20** depression
проглотить яд	**8** swallow poison		сахарный диабет	**21** diabetes
передозировка лекарства/ наркотика	**9** overdose on drugs		сердечное заболевание	**22** heart disease
падать–упал	**10** fall–fell		высокое давление/ гипертония	**23** high blood pressure/ hypertension
получать–получил удар током	**11** get–got an electric shock		туберкулёз лёгких	**24** TB/tuberculosis
грипп	**12** the flu/influenza		СПИД	**25** AIDS*
ушная инфекция	**13** an ear infection		* Синдром Приобретённого Иммунного Дефицита	* Acquired Immune Deficiency Syndrome

A. What happened?

B. My .... { is ___[1–3]___ .
has ___[4–5]___ .
is having a/an ___[6–7]___ .
___[8–11]___ed.

A. What's your location?
B. ....(address)........ .

A. My .... is sick.
B. What's the matter?
A. He/She has ___[12–25]___ .
B. I'm sorry to hear that.

Tell about a medical emergency that happened to you or someone you know.

Which illnesses in this lesson are you familiar with?

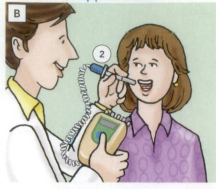

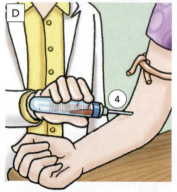

измерять *ваш* рост и вес	**A**	measure *your* height and weight	весы	**1** scale
измерять *вашу* температуру	**B**	take *your* temperature	градусник	**2** thermometer
измерять *ваше* давление	**C**	check *your* blood pressure	тонометр	**3** blood pressure gauge
брать анализ крови	**D**	draw some blood	игла/шприц	**4** needle/syringe
задавать вопросы о *вашем* здоровье	**E**	ask *you* some questions about *your* health	комната обследования	**5** examination room
проверять *ваши* глаза, уши, нос и горло	**F**	examine *your* eyes, ears, nose, and throat	диагностический стол/кушетка	**6** examination table
слушать *ваше* сердце	**G**	listen to *your* heart	оптометрическая таблица	**7** eye chart
сделать рентген грудной клетки	**H**	take a chest X-ray	стетоскоп	**8** stethoscope
			Рентгеновский аппарат	**9** X-ray machine

[A–H]
A. Now I'm going to **measure your height and weight**.
B. All right.

[A–H]
A. What did the doctor/nurse do during the examination?
B. She/He **measured my height and weight**.

[1–3, 5–9]
A. So, how do you like our new **scale?**
B. It's very nice, doctor.

How often do you have a medical exam? What does the doctor/nurse do?

МЕДИЦИНСКИЕ И СТОМАТОЛОГИЧЕСКИЕ ПРОЦЕДУРЫ

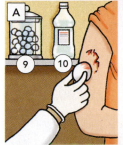 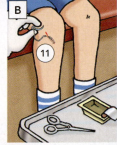 

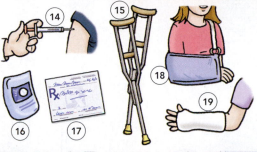

 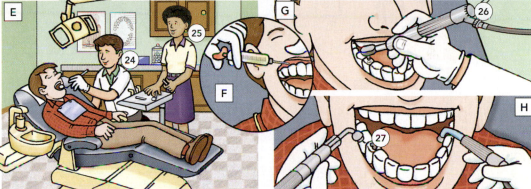

промывать рану	**A**	clean the wound
закрывать рану	**B**	close the wound
накладывать повязку	**C**	dress the wound
проводить чистку зубов	**D**	clean *your* teeth
проверять *ваши* зубы	**E**	examine *your* teeth
делать *укол* анестетика/ делать *укол* новокаина	**F**	give *you* a shot of anesthetic/ Novocaine™
сверлить больной зуб	**G**	drill the cavity
пломбировать зуб	**H**	fill the tooth

приёмная	**1**	waiting room
администратор	**2**	receptionist
карточка страхования	**3**	insurance card
анкета-история болезни	**4**	medical history form

комната обследования	**5**	examination room
врач/доктор/ терапевт	**6**	doctor/ physician
пациент	**7**	patient
медсестра	**8**	nurse
ватные тампоны	**9**	cotton balls
спирт	**10**	alcohol
швы	**11**	stitches
марля	**12**	gauze
лейкопластырь	**13**	tape
инъекция/ укол	**14**	injection/ shot
костыли	**15**	crutches

пузырь со льдом	**16**	ice pack
рецепт	**17**	prescription
поддерживающая повязка	**18**	sling
гипсовая повязка	**19**	cast
шина	**20**	brace
стоматолог- гигиенист	**21**	dental hygienist
маска	**22**	mask
перчатки	**23**	gloves
стоматолог	**24**	dentist
ассистент стоматолога	**25**	dental assistant
бормашина	**26**	drill
пломба	**27**	filling

A. Now I'm going to { ___[A–H]___.
  give you (a/an) ___[14–17]___.
  put your .... in a ___[18–20]___.

B. Okay.

A. I need { ___[9, 10, 12, 13, 23]___.
  a ___[22, 26]___.

B. Here you are.

Tell about a personal experience you had with a medical or dental procedure.

МЕДИЦИНСКИЕ РЕКОМЕНДАЦИИ

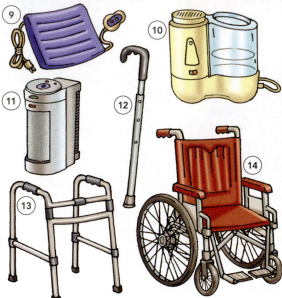

постельный режим	**1**	rest in bed	очиститель воздуха	**11** air purifier
пить много жидкости	**2**	drink fluids	трость	**12** cane
полоскать горло	**3**	gargle	ходунок (для инвалида)	**13** walker
сидеть на диете	**4**	go on a diet	инвалидное кресло	**14** wheelchair
заниматься спортом/делать зарядку	**5**	exercise	анализ крови/анализы крови	**15** blood work/blood tests
принимать витамины	**6**	take vitamins	анализы	**16** tests
идти на приём к специалисту	**7**	see a specialist	физиотерапия	**17** physical therapy
лечиться иглоукалыванием	**8**	get acupuncture	операция	**18** surgery
грелка	**9**	heating pad	консультация	**19** counseling
увлажнитель воздуха	**10**	humidifier	ортодонтические пластинки	**20** braces

A. I think { you should _____ [1–8] .
you should use a/an _____ [9–14] .
you need _____ [15–20] .

B. I see.

A. What did the doctor say?

B. The doctor thinks { I should _____ [1–8] .
I should use a/an _____ [9–14] .
I need _____ [15–20] .

Tell about medical advice a doctor gave you. What did the doctor say? Did you follow the advice?

ЛЕКАРСТВА

аспирин	**1**	aspirin
таблетки от простуды	**2**	cold tablets
витамины	**3**	vitamins
сироп от кашля	**4**	cough syrup
таблетки от боли	**5**	non-aspirin pain reliever
пастилки от кашля	**6**	cough drops
леденцы от боли в горле	**7**	throat lozenges
антацидные таблетки	**8**	antacid tablets
капли в нос	**9**	decongestant spray/ nasal spray
глазные капли	**10**	eye drops
мазь	**11**	ointment
крем	**12**	cream/creme
жидкий крем	**13**	lotion
драже	**14**	pill
таблетка	**15**	tablet
капсула	**16**	capsule
таблетка в форме капсулы	**17**	caplet
чайная ложка	**18**	teaspoon
столовая ложка	**19**	tablespoon

[1–13]

A. What did the doctor say?

B. { She / He told me to take _____ [1–4] _____ / a _____ [5] _____.
She / He told me to use _____ [6–13] _____.

[14–19]

A. What's the dosage?

B. One _____ every four hours.

What medicines in this lesson do you have at home? What other medicines do you have?

What do you take or use for a fever? a headache? a stomachache? a sore throat? a cold? a cough?

Tell about any medicines in your country that are different from the ones in this lesson.

ВРАЧИ-СПЕЦИАЛИСТЫ

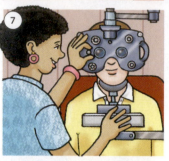

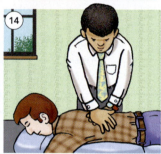
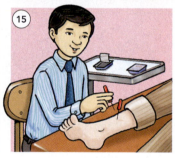

кардиолог	1	cardiologist
гинеколог	2	gynecologist
педиатр	3	pediatrician
геронтолог	4	gerontologist
аллерголог	5	allergist
ортопед	6	orthopedist
окулист	7	ophthalmologist
отоларинголог/ЛОР	8	ear, nose, and throat (ENT) specialist

сурдолог	9	audiologist
физиотерапевт	10	physical therapist
консультант/психолог	11	counselor/therapist
психиатр	12	psychiatrist
гастроэнтеролог	13	gastroenterologist
хиропрактик	14	chiropractor
иглотерапевт	15	acupuncturist
стоматолог	16	orthodontist

A. I think you need to see a specialist. I'm going to refer you to a/an _____.
B. A/An _____?
A. Yes.

A. When is your next appointment with the _____?
B. It's at ....(time)...... on .....(date).........

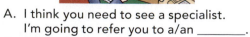

Do you or members of your family see any of these medical specialists? Which ones?

БОЛЬНИЦА

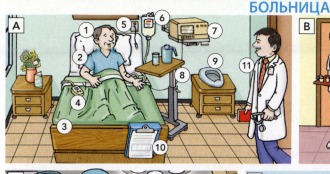

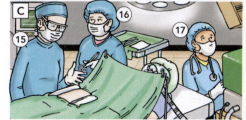

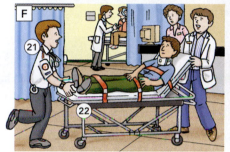

больничная палата	**A**	**patient's room**
пациент	1	patient
больничная пижама	2	hospital gown
больничная кровать	3	hospital bed
пульт управления кровати	4	bed control
кнопка вызова медсестры	5	call button
капельница	6	I.V.
монитор основных показателей	7	vital signs monitor
прикроватный столик	8	bed table
судно	9	bed pan
медицинская карта	10	medical chart
врач/доктор/терапевт	11	doctor/physician
пост медсестры	**B**	**nurse's station**
медсестра	12	nurse
диетолог	13	dietitian
санитар/больничный служитель	14	orderly
операционная	**C**	**operating room**
хирург	15	surgeon

хирургическая медсестра	16	surgical nurse
анестезиолог	17	anesthesiologist
комната ожидания	**D**	**waiting room**
помощник-доброволец	18	volunteer
родильная комната	**E**	**birthing room/delivery room**
акушер	19	obstetrician
акушер/медсестра-акушер	20	midwife/nurse-midwife
комната скорой помощи/ помещение скорой помощи	**F**	**emergency room/ ER**
сотрудник скорой помощи	21	emergency medical technician/EMT
каталка	22	gurney
рентгенологическое отделение	**G**	**radiology department**
рентген-лаборант	23	X-ray technician
рентгенолог	24	radiologist
лаборатория	**H**	**laboratory/lab**
лаборант	25	lab technician

A. This is your ____[2–10]____.
B. I see.

A. Do you work here?
B. Yes. I'm a/an ____[11–21, 23–25]____.

A. Where's the ____[11–21, 23–25]____?
B. She's/He's { in the ____[A, C–H]____.
   at the ____[B]____.

Tell about an experience you or a family member had in the hospital.

ЛИЧНАЯ ГИГИЕНА

A

B

C

D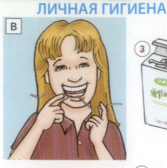

E

F

G

H

I

J

K

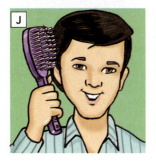

чистить зубы	**A**	**brush** *my* **teeth**
зубная щётка	**1**	toothbrush
зубная паста	**2**	toothpaste
пользоваться зубной ниткой	**B**	**floss** *my* **teeth**
зубная нить	**3**	dental floss
полоскать	**C**	**gargle**
ополаскиватель полости рта	**4**	mouthwash
отбеливать зубы	**D**	**whiten** *my* **teeth**
средство для отбеливания зубов	**5**	teeth whitener
принимать ванну	**E**	**bathe/take a bath**
мыло	**6**	soap
пена для ванн	**7**	bubble bath
принимать душ	**F**	**take a shower**
шапочка для душа	**8**	shower cap
мыть голову	**G**	**wash** *my* **hair**
шампунь	**9**	shampoo
кондиционер/ополаскиватель	**10**	conditioner/rinse

сушить волосы	**H**	**dry** *my* **hair**
фен	**11**	hair dryer/ blow dryer
причёсывать волосы	**I**	**comb** *my* **hair**
расчёска	**12**	comb
расчёсывать волосы	**J**	**brush** *my* **hair**
расчёска-щётка	**13**	(hair) brush
укладывать волосы	**K**	**style** *my* **hair**
плойка/ щипцы для завивки волос	**14**	hot comb/ curling iron
лак для волос	**15**	hairspray
гель для волос	**16**	hair gel
невидимка	**17**	bobby pin
заколка	**18**	barrette
заколка	**19**	hairclip

бриться	**L**	**shave**
крем для бритья	**20**	shaving cream
бритва	**21**	razor
лезвие бритвы	**22**	razor blade
электробритва	**23**	electric shaver
кровоостанавливающий карандаш	**24**	styptic pencil
лосьон после бритья	**25**	aftershave (lotion)
ухаживать за ногтями	**M**	**do my nails**
пилка	**26**	nail file
пилка	**27**	emery board
кусачки для ногтей	**28**	nail clipper
щётка для ногтей	**29**	nail brush
ножницы	**30**	scissors
лак для ногтей	**31**	nail polish
жидкость для снятия лака	**32**	nail polish remover
накладывать . . .	**N**	**put on . . .**
дезодорант	**33**	deodorant
крем для рук	**34**	hand lotion

крем для тела	**35**	body lotion
пудра	**36**	powder
одеколон/духи	**37**	cologne/perfume
солнцезащитный крем	**38**	sunscreen
накладывать косметику	**O**	**put on makeup**
румяна	**39**	blush/rouge
тональный крем	**40**	foundation/base
увлажняющий крем	**41**	moisturizer
пудра для лица	**42**	face powder
подводка	**43**	eyeliner
тени для век	**44**	eye shadow
тушь для ресниц	**45**	mascara
карандаш для бровей	**46**	eyebrow pencil
губная помада	**47**	lipstick
чистить ботинки	**P**	**polish my shoes**
крем для обуви	**48**	shoe polish
шнурки	**49**	shoelaces

[A–M, N (33–38), O, P]
A. What are you doing?
B. I'm _____ing.

[1, 8, 11–14, 17–19, 21–24, 26–30, 46, 49]
A. Excuse me. Where can I find _____(s)?
B. They're in the next aisle.

[2–7, 9, 10, 15, 16, 20, 25, 31–45, 47, 48]
A. Excuse me. Where can I find _____?
B. It's in the next aisle.

Which of these personal care products do you use?

You're going on a trip. Make a list of the personal care products you need to take with you.

УХОД ЗА РЕБЁНКОМ

кормить	**A feed**	ватная палочка	**15** cotton swab
детское питание	**1** baby food	детский крем	**16** baby lotion
слюнявчик	**2** bib		
бутылочка	**3** bottle	**держать**	**D hold**
соска	**4** nipple	соска	**17** pacifier
детская молочная смесь	**5** formula	детское зубное кольцо	**18** teething ring
жидкие витамины	**6** (liquid) vitamins		
		кормить грудью	**E nurse**
менять подгузник	**B change the baby's diaper**		
одноразовый подгузник	**7** disposable diaper	**одевать**	**F dress**
многоразовый подгузник	**8** cloth diaper		
булавка для подгузника	**9** diaper pin	**укачивать**	**G rock**
влажные салфетки	**10** (baby) wipes	ясли-сад	**19** child-care center
детская присыпка	**11** baby powder	сотрудник яслей-сада	**20** child-care worker
подгузник-трусики	**12** training pants	кресло-качалка	**21** rocking chair
мазь	**13** ointment		
		читать	**H read to**
купать	**C bathe**	вместилище игрушек	**22** cubby
детский шампунь	**14** baby shampoo		
		играть с	**I play with**
		игрушки	**23** toys

A. What are you doing?

B. { I'm _____[A, C–I]_____ ing the baby.
   { I'm _____[B]_____ ing.

A. Do we need anything from the store?

B. Yes. We need some more { _____[2–4, 7–9, 15, 17, 18]_____ s
   { _____[1, 5, 6, 10–14, 16]_____ .

In your opinion, which are better: cloth diapers or disposable diapers? Why?   Tell about baby products in your country.

ВИДЫ УЧЕБНЫХ ЗАВЕДЕНИЙ

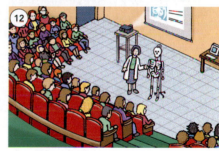

детский сад	**1**	preschool/nursery school
начальная школа	**2**	elementary school
средняя школа	**3**	middle school/ junior high school
старшие классы	**4**	high school
вечерняя школа	**5**	adult school
ПТУ	**6**	vocational school/trade school

местный колледж	**7**	community college
колледж	**8**	college
университет	**9**	university
аспирантура	**10**	graduate school
юридическая аспирантура	**11**	law school
медицинская аспирантура	**12**	medical school

A. Are you a student?
B. Yes. I'm in _____[1–4, 8, 10–12]_____.

A. Are you a student?
B. Yes. I go to a/an _____[5–7, 9]_____.

A. Is this apartment building near a/an _____?
B. Yes. ____(name of school)____ is nearby.

A. Tell me about your previous education.
B. I went to ____(name of school)____.
A. Did you like it there?
B. Yes. It was an excellent _____.

What types of schools are there in your community? What are their names, and where are they located?

What types of schools have you gone to?

Where? When? What did you study?

ШКОЛА

главное управление	**A**	(main) office		клерк/секретарь	**1**	clerk/
кабинет директора	**B**	principal's office		учебного заведения		(school) secretary
медицинский кабинет	**C**	nurse's office		директор	**2**	principal
кабинет советника	**D**	guidance office		медсестра	**3**	(school) nurse
класс	**E**	classroom		советник	**4**	(guidance) counselor
коридор	**F**	hallway		учитель	**5**	teacher
шкафчик		**a** locker		помощник директора/	**6**	assistant principal/
научная лаборатория	**G**	science lab		заместитель директора		vice-principal
спортзал	**H**	gym/gymnasium		охранник	**7**	security officer
раздевалка		**a** locker room		учитель области науки	**8**	science teacher
дорожка	**I**	track		учитель физкультуры	**9**	P.E. teacher
трибуны		**a** bleachers		тренер	**10**	coach
поле	**J**	field		уборщик	**11**	custodian
зал	**K**	auditorium		сотрудник столовой	**12**	cafeteria worker
столовая	**L**	cafeteria		смотритель столовой	**13**	lunchroom monitor
библиотека	**M**	library		библиотекарь	**14**	(school) librarian

A. Where are you going?
B. I'm going to the ___[A–D, G–M]___ .
A. Do you have a hall pass?
B. Yes. Here it is.

A. Where's the ___[1–14]___ ?
B. He's/She's in the ___[A–M]___ .

Describe the school where you study English.
Tell about the rooms, offices, and people.

Tell about differences between the school
in this lesson and schools in your country.

ШКОЛЬНЫЕ ПРЕДМЕТЫ

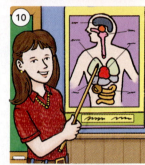

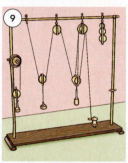
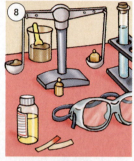

математика	**1** math/mathematics	информатика	**11** computer science
Английский язык	**2** English	Испанский язык	**12** Spanish
история	**3** history	Французский язык	**13** French
география	**4** geography	домоводство	**14** home economics
государство	**5** government	труд	**15** industrial arts/shop
естественные науки	**6** science	делопроизводство	**16** business education
биология	**7** biology	физкультура	**17** physical education/P.E.
химия	**8** chemistry	вождение	**18** driver's education/driver's ed
физика	**9** physics	изобразительное искусство	**19** art
охрана здоровья	**10** health	музыка	**20** music

A. What do you have next period?
B. **Math**. How about you?
A. **English**.
B. There's the bell. I've got to go.

What is/was your favorite subject? Why?

In your opinion, what's the most interesting subject? the most difficult subject? Why do you think so?

EXTRACURRICULAR ACTIVITIES

ШКОЛЬНЫЕ КРУЖКИ

группа	**1**	band	стенгазета/школьная газета	**9** school newspaper
оркестр	**2**	orchestra	ежегодник	**10** yearbook
хор	**3**	choir/chorus	литературный журнал	**11** literary magazine
драмкружок	**4**	drama	команда по звуку и освещению сцены	**12** A.V. crew
американский футбол	**5**	football	клуб дискуссий	**13** debate club
черлидинг/группа поддержки	**6**	cheerleading/pep squad	компьютерный клуб	**14** computer club
студенческий совет	**7**	student government	международный клуб	**15** international club
общественная работа	**8**	community service	шахматный клуб	**16** chess club

A. Are you going home right after school?

B. { No. I have _____[1–6]_____ practice.
{ No. I have a _____[7–16]_____ meeting.

What extracurricular activities do/did you participate in?

Which extracurricular activities in this lesson are there in schools in your country? What other activities are there?

МАТЕМАТИКА

Arithmetic   Арифметика

$$2+1=3 \qquad 8-3=5 \qquad 4\times2=8 \qquad 10\div2=5$$

сложение addition
2 **plus** 1 **equals*** 3.

вычитание subtraction
8 **minus** 3 **equals*** 5.

умножение multiplication
4 **times** 2 **equals*** 8.

деление division
10 **divided by** 2 **equals*** 5.

*You can also say: **is**

A. How much is *two plus one*?
B. *Two plus one* equals/is *three*.

Make conversations for the arithmetic problems above and others.

Fractions   Дробь

one quarter/
one fourth

one third

one half/
half

two thirds

three quarters/
three fourths

A. Is this on sale?
B. Yes. It's _____ off
the regular price.

A. Is the gas tank almost empty?
B. It's about _____ full.

Percents   Проценты

10%
ten
percent

50%
fifty
percent

75%
seventy-five
percent

100%
one-hundred
percent

A. How did you do on the test?
B. I got _____ percent of the
answers right.

A. What's the weather forecast?
B. There's a _____ percent
chance of rain.

Types of Math   Разделы математики

$$5y-5y+3=$$

$$sin\,(y)=x$$

$$\int_{2}^{6} g(x)\,dx$$

statistics
статистика

algebra
алгебра

geometry
геометрия

trigonometry
тригонометрия

calculus
исчисление

A. What math course are you taking this year?
B. I'm taking _____.

Are you good at math?

What math courses do/did
you take in school?

Tell about something you bought on sale.
How much off the regular price was it?

Research and discuss: What percentage
of people in your country live in cities?
live on farms? work in factories?
vote in general elections?

ИЗМЕРЕНИЯ И ГЕОМЕТРИЧЕСКИЕ ФИГУРЫ

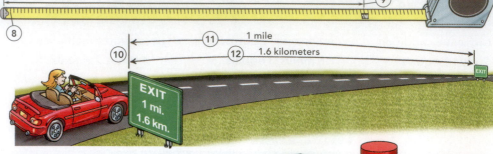

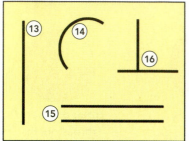

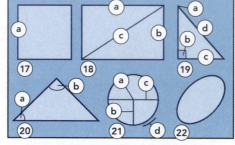

Измерения / Measurements

высота	1	height
ширина	2	width
глубина	3	depth
длина	4	length
дюйм	5	inch
фут–фит	6	foot–feet
ярд	7	yard
сантиметр	8	centimeter
метр	9	meter
расстояние	10	distance
миля	11	mile
километр	12	kilometer

Линии / Lines

прямая линия	13	straight line
кривая линия	14	curved line

параллельные прямые	15	parallel lines
перпендикулярные прямые	16	perpendicular lines

Геометрические Формы / Geometric Shapes

квадрат	17	square
сторона	a	side
прямоугольник	18	rectangle
длина	a	length
ширина	b	width
диагональ	c	diagonal
прямоугольный треугольник	19	right triangle
вершина	a	apex
прямой угол	b	right angle
основание	c	base
гипотенуза	d	hypotenuse

равнобедренный треугольник	20	isosceles triangle
острый угол	a	acute angle
тупой угол	b	obtuse angle
круг	21	circle
центр	a	center
радиус	b	radius
диаметр	c	diameter
окружность круга	d	circumference
эллипс/овал	22	ellipse/oval

Цельные Фигуры / Solid Figures

куб	23	cube
цилиндр	24	cylinder
шар	25	sphere
конус	26	cone
пирамида	27	pyramid

[1–9]
A. What's the _____ [1–4] ?
B. .... _____ [5–9] (s).

[11–12]
A. What's the distance?
B. .... _____(s).

1 inch (1") = 2.54 centimeters (cm)
1 foot (1') = 0.305 meters (m)
1 yard (1 yd.) = 0.914 meters (m)
1 mile (mi.) = 1.6 kilometers (km)

[17–22]
A. Who can tell me what shape this is?
B. I can. It's a/an _____.

[23–27]
A. Who knows what figure this is?
B. I do. It's a/an _____.

[13–27]
A. This painting is magnificent!
B. Hmm. I don't think so. It just looks like a lot of _____s and _____s to me!

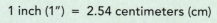

АНГЛИЙСКИЙ ЯЗЫК И СОЧИНЕНИЕ

Types of Sentences & Parts of Speech   **Виды Предложений и Части Речи**

A *Students study in the new library.*
① ② ③ ④ ⑤

C *Read page nine.*

B *Do they study hard?*
⑥ ⑦

D *This cake is fantastic!*

повествовательное	**A** declarative	имя существительное	**1** noun	имя прилагательное	**5** adjective
вопросительное	**B** interrogative	глагол	**2** verb	местоимение	**6** pronoun
повелительное	**C** imperative	предлог	**3** preposition	наречие	**7** adverb
восклицательное	**D** exclamatory	артикль	**4** article		

We study English every day.

A. What type of sentence is this?
B. It's a/an ___[A–D]___ sentence.

The student is tired.

A. What part of speech is this?
B. It's a/an ___[1–7]___.

Punctuation Marks & the Writing Process   Знаки Препинания и Сочинение

⑧ .   ⑨ ?   ⑩ !   ⑪ ,   ⑫ '   ⑬ " "   ⑭ :   ⑮ ;

⑯ moved   school   born

⑰ 1. born   2. moved   3. school

⑱ ⓐ My Life   ⓑ I was born in 1990 in Miami. I was the first child.

⑲ My Childhood / My Life ^   I was born in 1990 in Miami. I was the first child in my family

⑳

㉑ My Childhood / My Life ^   I was born in 1990 in Miami. I was the first child. in my family   My Childhood   I was born in Miami in 1990.

точка	**8** period	собрать свои идеи	**17** organize *my* ideas
вопросительный знак	**9** question mark	писать на черновике	**18** write a first draft
восклицательный знак	**10** exclamation point	заголовок	**a** title
запятая	**11** comma	параграф	**b** paragraph
апостроф	**12** apostrophe	исправлять	**19** make corrections/revise/edit
кавычки	**13** quotation marks	получать отзыв	**20** get feedback
двоеточие	**14** colon	переписывать на чистовик/	**21** write a final copy/
точка с запятой	**15** semi-colon	переписывать	rewrite
мыслить и записывать идеи	**16** brainstorm ideas		

A. Did you find any mistakes?
B. Yes. You forgot to put a/an ___[8–15]___ in this sentence.

A. Are you working on your composition?
B. Yes. I'm ___[16–21]___ing.

ЛИТЕРАТУРА И НАПИСАНИЕ

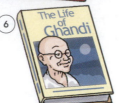

художественная литература	**1**	fiction
роман	**2**	novel
рассказ	**3**	short story
стихотворения/поэмы	**4**	poetry/poems
научная/документальная литература	**5**	non-fiction
биография	**6**	biography
автобиография	**7**	autobiography
сочинение	**8**	essay
доклад	**9**	report
журнальная статья	**10**	magazine article
газетная статья	**11**	newspaper article
редакционная статья	**12**	editorial
письмо	**13**	letter
открытка	**14**	postcard
записка	**15**	note
приглашение	**16**	invitation
благодарственное письмо	**17**	thank-you note
мемморандум	**18**	memo
электронная почта	**19**	e-mail
быстрое сообщение	**20**	instant message

A. What are you doing?

B. I'm writing { ____[1, 4, 5]____ .
a/an ____[2, 3, 6–20]____ .

What kind of literature do you like to read? What are some of your favorite books? Who is your favorite author?

Do you like to read newspapers and magazines? Which ones do you read?

Do you sometimes send or receive letters, postcards, notes, e-mail, or instant messages? Tell about the people you communicate with, and how.

ГЕОГРАФИЯ

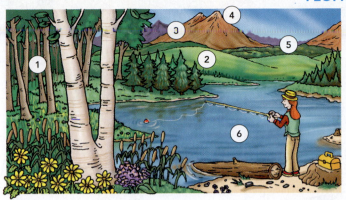

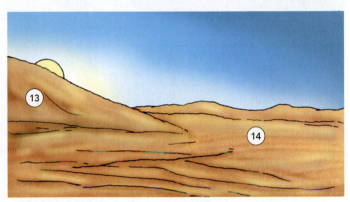
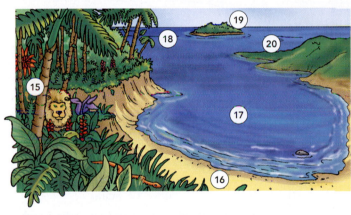
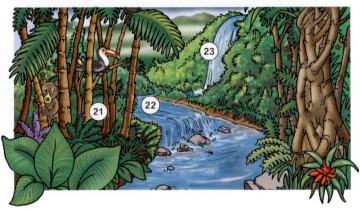

лес/роща	**1**	forest/woods	ручей/ручеёк	**9**	stream/brook	залив	**17**	bay
холм	**2**	hill	пруд	**10**	pond	океан	**18**	ocean
горная цепь	**3**	mountain range	плоскогорье	**11**	plateau	остров	**19**	island
вершина горы	**4**	mountain peak	глубокое ущелье/каньон	**12**	canyon	полуостров	**20**	peninsula
долина	**5**	valley	дюна/бархан	**13**	dune/sand dune	тропический лес	**21**	rainforest
озеро	**6**	lake	пустыня	**14**	desert	река	**22**	river
поля	**7**	plains	джунгли	**15**	jungle	водопад	**23**	waterfall
луг	**8**	meadow	морское побережье/берег	**16**	seashore/shore			

A. { Isn't this a beautiful _____?!
    Aren't these beautiful _____s?!
B.   Yes. It's / They're magnificent!

Tell about the geography of your country.
Describe the different geographic features.

Have you seen some of the geographic
features in this lesson? Which ones? Where?

НАУКА

Лабораторное Оборудование — Science Equipment

микроскоп	**1** microscope
компьютер	**2** computer
предметное стекло	**3** slide
чашка Петри	**4** Petri dish
колба	**5** flask
воронка	**6** funnel
мензурка	**7** beaker
пробирка	**8** test tube
зажим	**9** forceps
щипцы для тигля	**10** crucible tongs
горелка Бунзена	**11** Bunsen burner
измерительный цилиндр	**12** graduated cylinder
магнит	**13** magnet

призма	**14** prism
пипетка	**15** dropper
химикаты	**16** chemicals
весы	**17** balance
весы	**18** scale

Научный Метод — The Scientific Method

задавать задачу	**A** state the problem
формировать гипотезу	**B** form a hypothesis
планировать порядок действий	**C** plan a procedure
проводить процедуру	**D** do a procedure
вести наблюдения/ записывать наблюдения	**E** make/record observations
делать вывод	**F** draw conclusions

A. What do we need to do this procedure?
B. We need a/an/the ____[1–18]____.

A. How is your experiment coming along?
B. I'm getting ready to ____[A–F]____.

Do you have experience with the scientific equipment in this lesson? Tell about it.

What science courses do/did you take in school?

Think of an idea for a science experiment.
What question about science do you want to answer? State the problem.
What do you think will happen in the experiment? Form a hypothesis.
How can you test your hypothesis? Plan a procedure.

ВСЕЛЕННАЯ

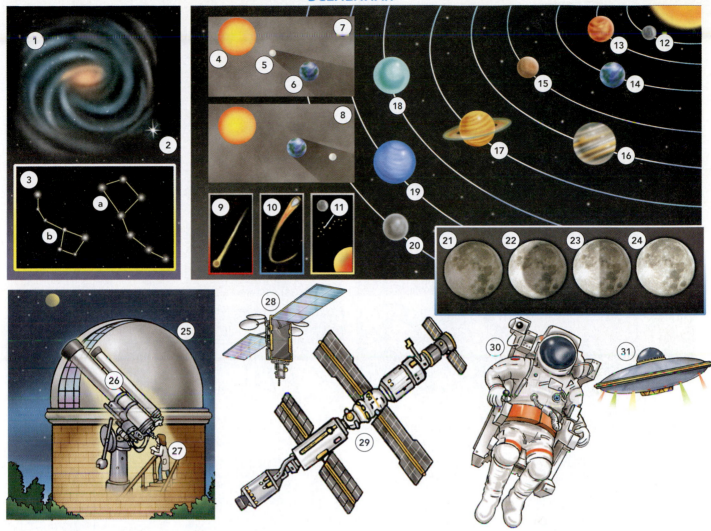

Вселенная	The Universe				
галактика	**1** galaxy	астероид	**11** asteroid	**Астрономия**	**Astronomy**
звезда	**2** star	Меркурий	**12** Mercury	обсерватория	**25** observatory
созвездие	**3** constellation	Венера	**13** Venus	телескоп	**26** telescope
Большая Медведица	**a** The Big Dipper	Земля	**14** Earth	астроном	**27** astronomer
Малая Медведица	**b** The Little Dipper	Марс	**15** Mars		
		Юпитер	**16** Jupiter	**Космонавтика**	**Space Exploration**
Солнечная Система	**The Solar System**	Сатурн	**17** Saturn	спутник	**28** satellite
солнце	**4** sun	Уран	**18** Uranus	космическая станция	**29** space station
луна	**5** moon	Нептун	**19** Neptune	астронавт/космонавт	**30** astronaut
планета	**6** planet	Плутон	**20** Pluto	НЛО/	**31** U.F.O./
солнечное затмение	**7** solar eclipse	новолуние	**21** new moon	Неопознанный	Unidentified
лунное затмение	**8** lunar eclipse	полумесяц	**22** crescent moon	Летающий Объект/	Flying Object/
метеор	**9** meteor	четверть луны	**23** quarter moon	летающая тарелка	flying saucer
комета	**10** comet	полнолуние	**24** full moon		

[1–24]
A. Is that (a/an/the) _____?
B. I'm not sure. I think it might be (a/an/the) _____.

[28–30]
A. Is the _____ ready for tomorrow's launch?
B. Yes. "All systems are go!"

Pretend you are an astronaut traveling in space. What do you see?

Draw and name a constellation you are familiar with.

Do you think space exploration is important? Why?

Have you ever seen a U.F.O.? Do you believe there is life in outer space? Why?

ПРОФЕССИИ I

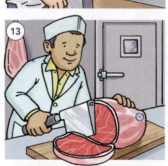

What's the problem?

бухгалтер	**1**	accountant	мясник	**13** butcher
актёр	**2**	actor	плотник	**14** carpenter
актриса	**3**	actress	кассир	**15** cashier
архитектор	**4**	architect	шеф-повар/повар	**16** chef/cook
художник	**5**	artist	сотрудник детского сада	**17** child day-care worker
сборщик	**6**	assembler	программист	**18** computer software engineer
приходящая няня	**7**	babysitter	рабочий-строитель	**19** construction worker
пекарь	**8**	baker	уборщик	**20** custodian/janitor
парикмахер	**9**	barber	представитель службы	**21** customer service
каменщик	**10**	bricklayer/mason	сервиса для клиентов	representative
предприниматель/бизнесмен	**11**	businessman	оператор по вводу данных	**22** data entry clerk
женщина-бизнесмен	**12**	businesswoman		

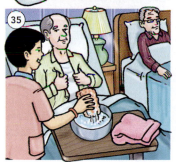

доставщик	**23**	delivery person	начальник цеха	**31**	foreman
портовый грузчик	**24**	dockworker	садовник/ландшафтник	**32**	gardener/landscaper
инженер	**25**	engineer	работник на фабрике одежды	**33**	garment worker
заводской рабочий	**26**	factory worker	парикмахер	**34**	hairdresser
фермер	**27**	farmer	медицинский сотрудник/санитар	**35**	health-care aide/attendant
пожарник	**28**	firefighter	сиделка/помощник	**36**	home health aide/
рыбак	**29**	fisher	по дому		home attendant
сотрудник	**30**	food-service	домработница	**37**	homemaker
продовольственной службы		worker	гостиничная уборщица	**38**	housekeeper

A. What do you do?
B. I'm an **accountant**. How about you?
A. I'm a **carpenter**.

[At a job interview]

A. Are you an experienced _____?
B. Yes. I'm a very experienced _____.

A. How long have you been a/an _____?
B. I've been a/an _____ for .... months/years.

Which of these occupations do you think are the most interesting? the most difficult? Why?

ПРОФЕССИИ II

журналист/корреспондент	**1** journalist/reporter
адвокат	**2** lawyer
станочник	**3** machine operator
почтальон	**4** mail carrier/letter carrier
руководитель	**5** manager
маникюрша	**6** manicurist
механик	**7** mechanic
помощник врача/ фельдшер	**8** medical assistant/ physician assistant
курьер	**9** messenger/courier
грузчик мебели	**10** mover

музыкант	**11** musician
маляр	**12** painter
фармаколог	**13** pharmacist
фотограф	**14** photographer
пилот	**15** pilot
полицейский	**16** police officer
почтовый работник	**17** postal worker
администратор	**18** receptionist
мастер по ремонту	**19** repairperson
продавец	**20** salesperson

мусорщик	**21**	sanitation worker/ trash collector	учитель/преподаватель	**30**	teacher/instructor
секретарь	**22**	secretary	продавец по телефону/ телемаркетолог	**31**	telemarketer
охранник	**23**	security guard	переводчик	**32**	translator/interpreter
военнослужащий	**24**	serviceman	турагент	**33**	travel agent
военнослужащая	**25**	servicewoman	водитель грузовика	**34**	truck driver
складской служащий	**26**	stock clerk	ветеринар	**35**	veterinarian/vet
владелец магазина	**27**	store owner/shopkeeper	официант	**36**	waiter/server
руководитель	**28**	supervisor	официантка	**37**	waitress/server
портной	**29**	tailor	сварщик	**38**	welder

A. What's your occupation?
B. I'm a **journalist**.
A. A **journalist**?
B. Yes. That's right.

A. Are you still a _____?
B. No. I'm a _____.
A. Oh. That's interesting.

A. What kind of job would you like in the future?
B. I'd like to be a _____.

Do you work? What's your occupation?

What are the occupations of people in your family?

РАБОЧИЕ НАВЫКИ И ЗАНЯТИЯ

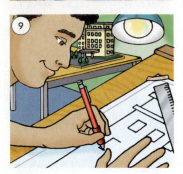

играть	**1** act	водить *грузовик*	**11** drive *a truck*
собирать *детали*	**2** assemble *components*	раскладывать	**12** file
помогать *больным*	**3** assist *patients*	управлять *самолётом*	**13** fly *an airplane*
печь	**4** bake	выращивать *овощи*	**14** grow *vegetables*
строить *вещи*/конструировать *вещи*	**5** build *things*/construct *things*	охранять *здания*	**15** guard *buildings*
убираться	**6** clean	управлять *рестораном*	**16** manage *a restaurant*
готовить	**7** cook	косить *газоны*	**17** mow *lawns*
доставлять *пиццу*	**8** deliver *pizzas*	управлять *оборудованием*	**18** operate *equipment*
создавать *архитектурные проекты*	**9** design *buildings*	красить	**19** paint
чертить	**10** draw	играть на *пианино*	**20** play the *piano*

готовить *еду*	**21**	prepare *food*
ремонтировать *вещи*/	**22**	repair *things*/
чинить *вещи*		fix *things*
продавать *машины*	**23**	sell *cars*
подавать *еду*	**24**	serve *food*
шить	**25**	sew
петь	**26**	sing
говорить на *испанском языке*	**27**	speak *Spanish*
руководить *людьми*	**28**	supervise *people*

заботиться о *престарелых*	**29**	take care of *elderly people*
проводить инвентаризацию	**30**	take inventory
преподавать	**31**	teach
переводить	**32**	translate
печатать	**33**	type
пользоваться *кассовым*	**34**	use *a cash register*
аппаратом		
мыть *посуду*	**35**	wash *dishes*
писать	**36**	write

A. Can you **act**?
B. Yes, I can.

A. Do you know how to _____?
B. Yes. I've been _____ing for years.

A. Tell me about your skills.
B. I can _____, and I can _____.

Tell about your job skills.
What can you do?

ПОИСК РАБОТЫ

Виды Объявлений на Работу	Types of Job Ads
вывеска-объявление о приёме на работу	1 help wanted sign
объявление о вакансии	2 job notice/ job announcement
рубричная реклама/ объявления о найме	3 classified ad/ want ad

сокращения в объявлениях о приёме на работу	Job Ad Abbreviations
полная ставка	4 full-time
не полная ставка	5 part-time
в наличии	6 available
час	7 hour
с Понедельника по Пятницу	8 Monday through Friday
вечера	9 evenings
предыдущий	10 previous
опыт	11 experience
обязателен	12 required

отличная	13	excellent

поиск работы	Job Search
отвечать на объявление	A respond to an ad
запрашивать информацию	B request information
попроситься на собеседование	C request an interview
подготовить резюме	D prepare a resume
правильно одеться	E dress appropriately
заполнить анкету	F fill out an application (form)
идти на собеседование	G go to an interview
рассказывать о своих навыках и квалификациях	H talk about your skills and qualifications
рассказывать о своём опыте	I talk about your experience
спрашивать о зарплате	J ask about the salary
спрашивать о предоставляемых льготах	K ask about the benefits
писать благодарственное письмо	L write a thank-you note
получить работу	M get hired

A. How did you find your job?
B. I found it through a ____[1–3]____.

A. How was your job interview?
B. It went very well.
A. Did you ____[D–F, H–M]____?
B. Yes, I did.

Tell about a job you are familiar with. What are the skills and qualifications required for the job? What are the hours? What is the salary?

Tell about how people you know found their jobs.

Tell about your own experience with a job search or a job interview.

НА РАБОТЕ

приёмная	**A**	reception area	штемпельная машина	**7**	postage meter	менеджер офиса	**23**	office manager
комната совещаний	**B**	conference room	ассистент (по офису)	**8**	office assistant	шкаф для канцтоваров	**24**	supply cabinet
почтовая комната	**C**	mailroom	почтовый ящик	**9**	mailbox	кладовка	**25**	storage cabinet
офисное помещение	**D**	work area	офисная перегородка	**10**	cubicle	автомат продажи напитков/закусок	**26**	vending machine
офис	**E**	office	офисный стул	**11**	swivel chair	охладитель воды	**27**	water cooler
комната офисных товаров	**F**	supply room	печатная машинка	**12**	typewriter	кофеварка	**28**	coffee machine
кладовая комната	**G**	storage room	счётная машина	**13**	adding machine	доска объявлений	**29**	message board
буфет/комната отдыха сотрудников	**H**	employee lounge	ксерокс	**14**	copier/photocopier	записать сообщение	**a**	take a message
вешалка	**1**	coat rack	шредер	**15**	paper shredder	выступать	**b**	give a presentation
гардероб	**2**	coat closet	бумагорезательный прибор	**16**	paper cutter	разбирать почту	**c**	sort the mail
администратор	**3**	receptionist	регистратор	**17**	file clerk	ксерокопировать	**d**	make copies
стол совещаний	**4**	conference table	шкаф с документами	**18**	file cabinet	раскладывать (документы)	**e**	file
доска для презентаций	**5**	presentation board	секретарь	**19**	secretary	печатать письмо	**f**	type a letter
почтовые весы	**6**	postal scale	компьютерный стол	**20**	computer workstation			
			начальник	**21**	employer/boss			
			помощник начальника	**22**	administrative assistant			

[A–H]
A. Where's .....(name)..... ?
B. He's / She's in the _____.

[1–29]
A. What do you think of the new _____?
B. He's / She's / It's very nice.

[a–f]
A. What's .....(name)..... doing?
B. He's / She's _____ing.

Describe a workplace you are familiar with. Tell about the rooms, the areas, and the employees.

КАНЦЕЛЯРСКИЕ ТОВАРЫ

стол (рабочий)	**1**	desk
сшиватель/степлер	**2**	stapler
лоток для бумаги	**3**	letter tray/ stacking tray
картотечный блокнот	**4**	rotary card file
настольная подкладка	**5**	desk pad
ежедневник	**6**	appointment book
зажим для бумаг	**7**	clipboard
блокнот	**8**	note pad/ memo pad
электрическая точилка	**9**	electric pencil sharpener
настольный календарь	**10**	desk calendar
блок для записей	**11**	Post-It note pad

органайзер/ блокнот	**12**	organizer/ personal planner
резинка	**13**	rubber band
скрепка	**14**	paper clip
скоба для степлера	**15**	staple
кнопка	**16**	thumbtack
кнопка	**17**	pushpin
блокнот в линейку	**18**	legal pad
папка	**19**	file folder
картотечная карточка	**20**	index card
конверт	**21**	envelope
бланк	**22**	stationery/ letterhead (paper)
конверт	**23**	mailer

почтовый ярлык	**24**	mailing label
лента для печатной машинки	**25**	typewriter cartridge
картридж	**26**	ink cartridge
печать	**27**	rubber stamp
штемпельная подушка	**28**	ink pad
клей-карандаш	**29**	glue stick
клей	**30**	glue
резиновый клей	**31**	rubber cement
штрих	**32**	correction fluid
скотч	**33**	cellophane tape/ clear tape
упаковочная клейкая лента	**34**	packing tape/ sealing tape

A. My desk is a mess! I can't find my __[2–12]__ !
B. Here it is next to your __[2–12]__ .

A. Could you get some more __[13–21, 23–29]__ s/ __[22, 30–34]__ from the supply room?
B. Some more __[13–21, 23–29]__ s/ __[22, 30–34]__ ? Sure. I'd be happy to.

Which supplies and equipment do you use? What do you use them for?

Which supplies in this lesson do you have at home? at school?

ФАБРИКА

табельные часы	1	time clock		вилочный погрузчик	13	forklift
карточка табельного учёта	2	time cards		грузовой лифт	14	freight elevator
раздевалка	3	locker room		объявление профсоюза	15	union notice
линия сборки	4	(assembly) line		ящик для предложений	16	suggestion box
заводской рабочий	5	(factory) worker		отдел отгрузки	17	shipping department
рабочее место	6	work station		экспедитор	18	shipping clerk
линия наблюдения	7	line supervisor		тележка	19	hand truck/dolly
контролёр качества	8	quality control supervisor		погрузочная платформа	20	loading dock
станок	9	machine		бухгалтерия/	21	payroll office
лента конвейера	10	conveyor belt		отдел начисления зарплаты		
склад	11	warehouse		отдел кадров	22	personnel office
упаковщик	12	packer				

A. Excuse me. I'm a new employee. Where's/Where are the _____?
B. Next to/Near/In/On the _____.

A. Have you seen *Tony*?
B. Yes. *He's* in/on/at/next to/near the _____.

Are there any factories where you live? What kind? What are the working conditions there?

What products do factories in your country produce?

СТРОЙПЛОЩАДКА

молот	**1**	sledgehammer	цементомешалка	**11**	cement mixer	пикап	**20** pickup truck
кирка	**2**	pickax	цемент	**a**	cement	прицеп/трейлер	**21** trailer
лопата	**3**	shovel	строительные леса	**12**	scaffolding	гипсокартон	**22** drywall
тачка	**4**	wheelbarrow	самосвал	**13**	dump truck	древесина	**23** wood/lumber
пневматический бурильный молоток	**5**	jackhammer/ pneumatic drill	фронтальный погрузчик	**14**	front-end loader	фанера	**24** plywood
план/ светокопия	**6**	blueprints	кран	**15**	crane	теплоизоляция	**25** insulation
лестница	**7**	ladder	автогидроподъёмник	**16**	cherry picker	провод	**26** wire
рулетка	**8**	tape measure	бульдозер	**17**	bulldozer	кирпич	**27** brick
пояс для инструментов	**9**	toolbelt	экскаватор	**18**	backhoe	гонт	**28** shingle
мастерок	**10**	trowel	бетоносмеситель	**19**	concrete mixer truck	труба	**29** pipe
			бетон	**a**	concrete	брус/балка	**30** girder/beam

A. Could you get me that/those ___[1–10]___ ?
B. Sure.

A. Watch out for that ___[11–21]___ !
B. Oh! Thanks for the warning!

A. Do we have enough ___[22–26]___ / ___[27–30]___ s?
B. I think so.

What building materials is your home made of?
When was it built?

Describe a construction site near your home or school.
Tell about the construction equipment and the materials.

ТЕХНИКА БЕЗОПАСНОСТИ

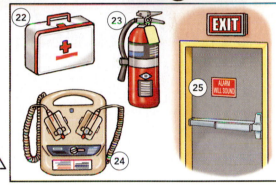

защитная каска	**1**	hard hat/helmet
беруши	**2**	earplugs
защитные очки	**3**	goggles
защитный жилет	**4**	safety vest
рабочие сапоги	**5**	safety boots
защитные насадки на обувь	**6**	toe guard
пояс-поддержка для спины	**7**	back support
защитные наушники	**8**	safety earmuffs

сеточка для волос	**9**	hairnet
маска	**10**	mask
резиновые перчатки	**11**	latex gloves
респиратор	**12**	respirator
защитные очки	**13**	safety glasses
огнеопасно	**14**	flammable
ядовито/токсично	**15**	poisonous
едкий/разъедающий	**16**	corrosive

радиоактивно	**17**	radioactive
опасно	**18**	dangerous
опасно	**19**	hazardous
биологически опасно	**20**	biohazard
опасность поражения электротоком	**21**	electrical hazard
аптечка	**22**	first-aid kit
огнетушитель	**23**	fire extinguisher
дефибриллятор	**24**	defibrillator
запасной выход	**25**	emergency exit

A. Don't forget to wear your ___[1–13]___!
B. Thanks for reminding me.

A. Be careful!
That material is ___[14–17]___!
That machine is ___[18]___!
That work area is ___[19]___!
That's a ___[20]___!/That's an ___[21]___!
B. Thanks for the warning.

A. Where's the ___[22–25]___?
B. It's over there.

Have you ever used any of the safety equipment in this lesson? What have you used? When? Where?

Where do you see people using safety equipment in your community?

ОБЩЕСТВЕННЫЙ ТРАНСПОРТ

автобус	**A**	**bus**
автобусная остановка	**1**	bus stop
маршрут автобуса	**2**	bus route
пассажир	**3**	passenger/rider
тариф на проезд в автобусе	**4**	(bus) fare
пересадочный билет	**5**	transfer
водитель автобуса	**6**	bus driver
автовокзал	**7**	bus station
билетный киоск	**8**	ticket counter
билет	**9**	ticket
багажное отделение	**10**	baggage compartment/ luggage compartment
поезд/электричка	**B**	**train**
вокзал	**11**	train station
билетная касса	**12**	ticket window

табло прибытия и отправления поездов	**13**	arrival and departure board
справочное бюро	**14**	information booth
расписание	**15**	schedule/ timetable
платформа	**16**	platform
рельсовый путь	**17**	track
проводник	**18**	conductor
метро	**C**	**subway**
станция метро	**19**	subway station
жетон	**20**	(subway) token
турникет	**21**	turnstile
проездной билет	**22**	fare card

автомат продажи проездных билетов	**23**	fare card machine
taxi	**D**	**taxi**
стоянка такси	**24**	taxi stand
такси	**25**	taxi/cab/ taxicab
счётчик такси	**26**	meter
таксист	**27**	cab driver/ taxi driver
теплоход	**E**	**ferry**

[A–E]
A. How are you going to get there?
B. { I'm going to take the __[A–C, E]__ .
{ I'm going to take a __[D]__ .

[1, 7, 8, 10–19, 21, 23–25]
A. Excuse me. Where's the _____?
B. Over there.

How do you get to different places in your community? Describe public transportation where you live.

In your country, can you travel far by train or by bus? Where can you go? How much do tickets cost? Describe the buses and trains.

ТИПЫ АВТОМОБИЛЕЙ

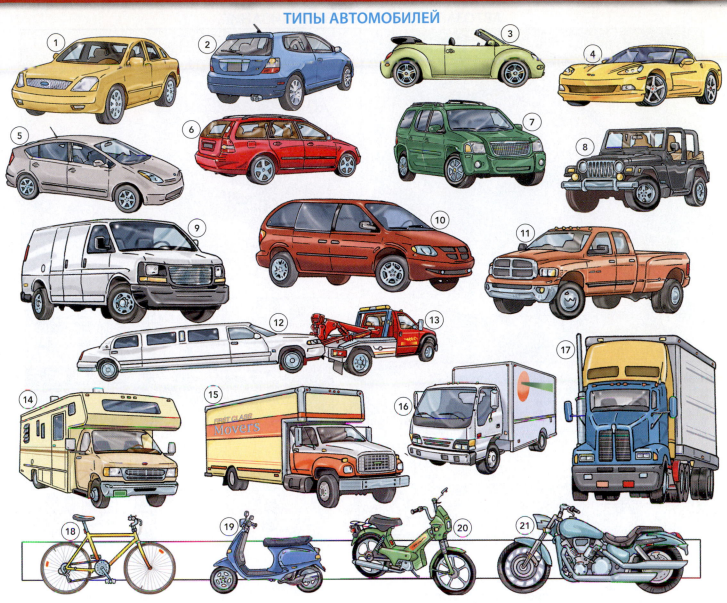

седан	**1**	sedan
хэтчбек/комби	**2**	hatchback
автомобиль с откидным верхом	**3**	convertible
спортивный автомобиль	**4**	sports car
автомобиль с гибридным двигателем	**5**	hybrid
автомобиль-универсал	**6**	station wagon
внедорожник	**7**	S.U.V. (sport utility vehicle)
джип	**8**	jeep
микроавтобус	**9**	van
микроавтобус	**10**	minivan
пикап	**11**	pickup truck

лимузин	**12**	limousine
автоэвакуатор	**13**	tow truck
жилой автофургон	**14**	R.V. (recreational vehicle)/camper
грузовик для перевозки мебели	**15**	moving van
грузовик	**16**	truck
грузовик с прицепом	**17**	tractor trailer/semi
велосипед	**18**	bicycle/bike
мотороллер/скутер	**19**	motor scooter
мопед	**20**	moped
мотоцикл	**21**	motorcycle

A. What kind of vehicle are you looking for?
B. I'm looking for a **sedan**.

A. Do you drive a/an _____?
B. No. I drive a/an _____.

A. I just saw an accident between a/an _____ and a/an _____!
B. Was anybody hurt?
A. No. Fortunately, nobody was hurt.

What are the most common types of vehicles in your country?

What's your favorite type of vehicle? Why? In your opinion, which company makes the best one?

АВТОЗАПЧАСТИ И ТЕХОБСЛУЖИВАНИЕ

бампер	1	bumper		домкрат	26	jack
фара	2	headlight		запасное колесо	27	spare tire
сигнал поворота	3	turn signal		гаечный ключ	28	lug wrench
стояночная фара	4	parking light		сигнал-вспышка	29	flare
крыло	5	fender		соединительный кабель	30	jumper cables
шина	6	tire		свечи зажигания	31	spark plugs
колпак	7	hubcap		воздухоочиститель (фильтр)	32	air filter
капот	8	hood		двигатель/мотор	33	engine
лобовое стекло	9	windshield		система впрыска топлива	34	fuel injection system
дворники	10	windshield wipers		радиатор	35	radiator
зеркало бокового обозрения	11	side mirror		шланг радиатора	36	radiator hose
багажник на крыше	12	roof rack		ремень вентилятора	37	fan belt
люк в крыше	13	sunroof		генератор	38	alternator
антенна	14	antenna		измерительный стержень	39	dipstick
заднее стекло	15	rear window		аккумулятор	40	battery
задний дефростер	16	rear defroster		насос	41	air pump
багажник	17	trunk		бензоколонка	42	gas pump
задняя фара	18	taillight		сопло	43	nozzle
тормозные огни	19	brake light		крышка бензобака	44	gas cap
огни заднего хода	20	backup light		бензин	45	gas
номерной знак	21	license plate		масло	46	oil
выхлопная труба	22	tailpipe/exhaust pipe		охлаждающая жидкость	47	coolant
глушитель	23	muffler		воздух	48	air
коробка передач	24	transmission				
бензобак	25	gas tank				

подушка безопасности	**49**	air bag	гудок	**60**	horn	автоматическая коробка передач	**74** automatic transmission
солнцезащитный щиток	**50**	visor	зажигание	**61**	ignition	рычаг коробки передач	**75** gearshift
зеркало заднего обзора	**51**	rearview mirror	вентиляционное отверстие	**62**	vent	коробка передач	**76** manual transmission
приборный щит	**52**	dashboard/ instrument panel	навигатор	**63**	navigation system	рычаг коробки передач	**77** stickshift
термометр	**53**	temperature gauge	радио	**64**	radio	сцепление	**78** clutch
измеритель топлива	**54**	gas gauge/ fuel gauge	CD плеер	**65**	CD player	дверной замок	**79** door lock
спидометр	**55**	speedometer	печка	**66**	heater	дверная ручка	**80** door handle
одометр	**56**	odometer	кондиционеры	**67**	air conditioning	плечевой ремень безопасности	**81** shoulder harness
предупредительные индикаторы	**57**	warning lights	дефростер	**68**	defroster	подлокотник	**82** armrest
сигнал поворота	**58**	turn signal	розетка	**69**	power outlet	подголовник	**83** headrest
руль	**59**	steering wheel	бардачок	**70**	glove compartment	сиденье	**84** seat
			запасной тормоз/ ручник	**71**	emergency brake	ремень безопасности	**85** seat belt
			тормоза	**72**	brake (pedal)		
			педаль газа	**73**	accelerator/ gas pedal		

[2, 3, 9–16, 24, 35–39, 49–85]

A. What's the matter with your car?
B. The _____(s) is/are broken.

[45–48]

A. Can I help you?
B. { Yes. My car needs _____[45–47]_____.
    { Yes. My tires need _____[48]_____.

[1, 2, 4–15, 17–23, 25]

A. I was just in a car accident!
B. Oh, no! Were you hurt?
A. No. But my _____(s) was/were damaged.

In your opinion, what are the most important features to look for when you buy a car?

Do you own a car? What kind? Tell about any repairs your car has needed.

ТРАССЫ И УЛИЦЫ

тоннель	**1**	tunnel
мост	**2**	bridge
касса платной дороги	**3**	tollbooth
дорожный указатель	**4**	route sign
трасса	**5**	highway
дорога	**6**	road
дорожный барьер	**7**	divider/ barrier
эстакада	**8**	overpass
проезд под эстакадой	**9**	underpass
въезд на трассу	**10**	entrance ramp/ on ramp

междуштатная трасса	**11**	interstate (highway)
разделяющая полоса	**12**	median
левая полоса	**13**	left lane
средняя полоса	**14**	middle lane/ center lane
правая полоса	**15**	right lane
обочина	**16**	shoulder
пунктирная линия	**17**	broken line
сплошная линия	**18**	solid line
знак ограничения скорости	**19**	speed limit sign
выезд	**20**	exit (ramp)
указатель на выезд с трассы	**21**	exit sign

улица	**22**	street
улица одностороннего движения	**23**	one-way street
двойная сплошная жёлтая линия	**24**	double yellow line
пешеходный переход	**25**	crosswalk
перекрёсток	**26**	intersection
светофор	**27**	traffic light/ traffic signal
угол	**28**	corner
квартал	**29**	block

[1–28]
A. Where's the accident?
B. It's on / in / at / near the _____.

Describe a highway you travel on.

Describe an intersection near where you live.

In your area, on which highways and streets do most accidents occur? Why are these places dangerous?

ПРЕДЛОГИ ДВИЖЕНИЯ

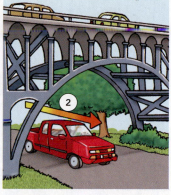

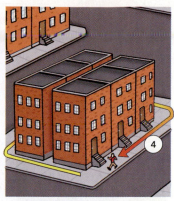

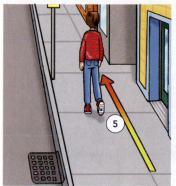

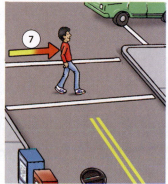
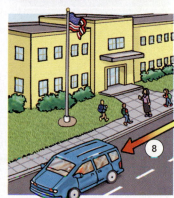

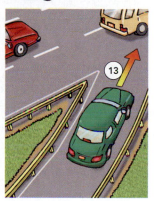

над/через	**1**	over
под	**2**	under
через/сквозь	**3**	through
вокруг	**4**	around

вверх по	**5**	up
вниз по	**6**	down
через	**7**	across
мимо	**8**	past

в/на	**9**	on
с/из	**10**	off
в	**11**	into
из	**12**	out of
на	**13**	onto

[1–8]
A. Go **over** the bridge.
B. **Over** the bridge?
A. Yes.

[9–13]
A. I can't talk right now. I'm getting **on** a train.
B. You're getting **on** a train?
A. Yes. I'll call you later.

What places do you go past on your way to school?   Tell how to get to different places from your home or your school.

ДОРОЖНЫЕ ЗНАКИ И НАПРАВЛЕНИЯ

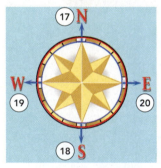

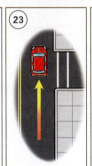
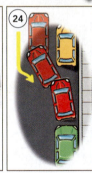

Дорожные Знаки	Traffic Signs
стоп	**1** stop
поворот налево запрещён	**2** no left turn
поворот направо запрещён	**3** no right turn
разворот запрещён	**4** no U-turn
поворот направо	**5** right turn only
въезд запрещён	**6** do not enter
выезд на дорогу с односторонним движением	**7** one way
конец дороги/тупик	**8** dead end/no outlet
пешеходный переход	**9** pedestrian crossing
железнодорожный переезд	**10** railroad crossing
осторожно дети	**11** school crossing

въезд на полосу	**12** merging traffic
уступите дорогу	**13** yield
объезд	**14** detour
скользкая дорога	**15** slippery when wet
стоянка для инвалидов	**16** handicapped parking only

Компасные Направления / **Compass Directions**

север	**17** north
юг	**18** south
запад	**19** west
восток	**20** east

Задания на Экзамене Вождения / **Road Test Instructions**

Повернитесь налево.	**21** Turn left.
Повернитесь направо.	**22** Turn right.
Езжайте прямо.	**23** Go straight.
Припаркуйтесь параллельно.	**24** Parallel park.
Развернитесь в три приёма.	**25** Make a 3-point turn.
Используйте ручные сигналы.	**26** Use hand signals.

[1–16]
A. Careful! That sign says "**stop**"!
B. Oh. Thanks.

[17–20]
A. Which way should I go?
B. Go **north**.

[21–26]
A. Turn **right**.
B. Turn **right**?
A. Yes.

Which of these traffic signs are in your neighborhood?
What other traffic signs do you usually see?

Describe any differences between traffic signs in different countries you know.

АЭРОПОРТ

Регистрация		A Check-In		Зона Выдачи Багажа		D Baggage Claim
билет	**1**	ticket		зона выдачи багажа	**15**	baggage claim (area)
билетная касса	**2**	ticket counter		транспортёр выдачи багажа	**16**	baggage carousel
кассир билетной кассы	**3**	ticket agent		багаж	**17**	baggage
чемодан	**4**	suitcase		тележка для багажа	**18**	baggage cart/ luggage cart
табло прилёта и вылета	**5**	arrival and departure monitor		раскладная тележка для багажа	**19**	luggage carrier
				складной саквояж	**20**	garment bag
Охрана		**B Security**		ярлык для багажа	**21**	baggage claim check
контрольно-пропускной пункт	**6**	security checkpoint				
металлодетектор	**7**	metal detector		**Таможенный и Иммиграционный Контроль**		**E Customs and Immigration**
охранник	**8**	security officer		таможенный контроль	**22**	customs
рентгеновская установка	**9**	X-ray machine		таможенник	**23**	customs officer
ручная кладь	**10**	carry-on bag		таможенная декларация	**24**	customs declaration form
				иммиграционный контроль	**25**	immigration
Выход на Посадку		**C The Gate**		сотрудник иммиграционной службы	**26**	immigration officer
стойка регистрации пассажиров	**11**	check-in counter		паспорт	**27**	passport
посадочный талон	**12**	boarding pass		виза	**28**	visa
выход на посадку	**13**	gate				
зал ожидания пассажиров	**14**	boarding area				

[2, 3, 5–9, 11, 13–16, 22, 23, 25, 26]
A. Excuse me. Where's the _____?*
B. Right over there.

* With 22 and 25, use: Excuse me. Where's _____?

[1, 4, 10, 12, 17–21, 24, 27, 28]
A. Oh, no! I think I've lost my _____!
B. I'll help you look for it.

Describe an airport you are familiar with. Tell about the check-in area, the security area, the gates, and the baggage claim area.

Have you ever gone through Customs and Immigration? Tell about your experience.

АВИА ПУТЕШЕСТВИЯ

кабина экипажа	1	cockpit
пилот/первый пилот	2	pilot/captain
второй пилот	3	co-pilot
туалет	4	lavatory/bathroom
стюардесса/стюард	5	flight attendant
верхняя багажная полка	6	overhead compartment
проход	7	aisle
сиденье у окна	8	window seat
сиденье в середине	9	middle seat
сиденье у прохода	10	aisle seat
индикатор "пристегните ремни"	11	Fasten Seat Belt sign
индикатор "не курить"	12	No Smoking sign
кнопка вызова стюардессы	13	call button
кислородная маска	14	oxygen mask
запасной выход	15	emergency exit
раскладной столик	16	tray (table)
инструкции действий в аварийной обстановке	17	emergency instruction card
гигиенический пакет	18	air sickness bag

спасательный жилет	19	life vest/life jacket
взлётно-посадочная полоса	20	runway
терминал	21	terminal (building)
диспетчерская вышка	22	control tower
самолёт	23	airplane/plane/jet

Russian	Letter	English
снимать обувь	A	take off your shoes
достать все предметы из карманов	B	empty your pockets
положить сумку на конвейер	C	put your bag on the conveyor belt
поставить компьютер в лоток	D	put your computer in a tray
пройти через металлодетектор	E	walk through the metal detector
зарегистрироваться на посадку	F	check in at the gate
получить посадочный талон	G	get your boarding pass
заходить в самолёт	H	board the plane
поставить ручную кладь	I	stow your carry-on bag
найти своё место	J	find your seat
пристегнуться	K	fasten your seat belt

[1–23]
A. Where's the _____?
B. In/On/Next to/Behind/In front of/ Above/Below the _____.

[A–K]
A. Please _____.
B. All right. Certainly.

Have you ever flown in an airplane? Tell about a flight you took.

Be an airport security officer! Give passengers instructions as they go through the security area. Now, be a flight attendant! Give passengers instructions before take-off.

ГОСТИНИЦА

портье/швейцар	1	doorman	стойка регистрации	8	front desk	машина изготовления льда	19	ice machine
услуги парковки	2	valet parking	администратор	9	desk clerk	коридор	20	hall/hallway
сотрудник парковки	3	parking attendant	постоялец	10	guest	магнитный ключ-карточка	21	room key
посыльный	4	bellhop	стол консьержа	11	concierge desk	тележка уборщицы	22	housekeeping cart
тележка для багажа	5	luggage cart	консьерж	12	concierge	уборщица	23	housekeeper
старший посыльный	6	bell captain	ресторан	13	restaurant	номер	24	guest room
вестибюль	7	lobby	зал заседаний	14	meeting room	обслуживание номеров	25	room service
			магазин сувениров	15	gift shop			
			бассейн	16	pool			
			спортзал	17	exercise room			
			лифт	18	elevator			

A. Where do you work?
B. I work at the *Grand* Hotel.
A. What do you do there?
B. I'm a/an _____ [1, 3, 4, 6, 9, 12, 23] .

A. Excuse me. Where's the _____ [1–19, 22, 23] ?
B. Right over there.
A. Thanks.

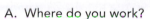 Tell about a hotel you are familiar with. Describe the place and the people.

 In your opinion, which hotel employee has the most interesting job? the most difficult job? Why?

ХОББИ, РУКОДЕЛИЕ И ИГРЫ

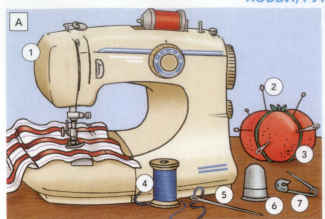

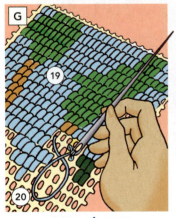

шить	**A sew**
швейная машинка	**1** sewing machine
булавка	**2** pin
подушечка для булавок	**3** pin cushion
катушка ниток	**4** (spool of) thread
иголка	**5** (sewing) needle
напёрсток	**6** thimble
английская булавка	**7** safety pin
вязать спицами	**B knit**
спица	**8** knitting needle
пряжа	**9** yarn
вязать крючком	**C crochet**
крючок	**10** crochet hook

рисовать красками	**D paint**
кисть	**11** paintbrush
мольберт	**12** easel
холст	**13** canvas
краска	**14** paint
масляная краска	**a** oil paint
акварельные краски	**b** watercolor
рисовать карандашом	**E draw**
альбом	**15** sketch book
набор цветных карандашей	**16** (set of) colored pencils
рисовальный карандаш	**17** drawing pencil
вышивать	**F do embroidery**
вышивание	**18** embroidery
вышивать по канве	**G do needlepoint**
вышивание по канве	**19** needlepoint
канва	**20** pattern

работать с деревом	**H do woodworking**
набор для работы по дереву	**21** woodworking kit
складывать оригами	**I do origami**
бумага для оригами	**22** origami paper
заниматься керамикой	**J make pottery**
глина	**23** clay
гончарный станок	**24** potter's wheel

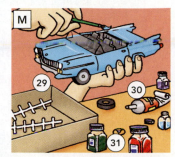

коллекционировать марки	**K**	**collect stamps**
альбом с марками	25	stamp album
лупа	26	magnifying glass
коллекционировать монеты	**L**	**collect coins**
каталог монет	27	coin catalog
альбом для монет	28	coin collection
строить модели	**M**	**build models**
набор сбора модели	29	model kit
клей	30	glue
акриловая краска	31	acrylic paint
наблюдать за птицами	**N**	**go bird-watching**
бинокль	32	binoculars

зоологический справочник	33	field guide
играть в карты	**O**	**play cards**
колода карт	34	(deck of) cards
трефы	**a**	club
буби/бубны	**b**	diamond
черви	**c**	heart
пики	**d**	spade
играть в настольные игры	**P**	**play board games**
шахматы	35	chess
шашки	36	checkers
нарды	37	backgammon

Монополия	38	Monopoly
кубики	**a**	dice
игра в слова	39	Scrabble
сидеть в интернете	**Q**	**go online/ browse the Web/ "surf" the net**
веб-браузер	40	web browser
адрес сайта	41	web address/URL
фотография	**R**	**photography**
фотоаппарат	42	camera
астрономия	**S**	**astronomy**
телескоп	43	telescope

A. What do you like to do in your free time?
B. I like to ____[A–Q]____ .
I enjoy ____[R, S]____ .

A. May I help you?
B. Yes, please. I'd like to buy (a/an) ____[1–34, 42, 43]____ .

A. What do you want to do?
B. Let's play ____[35–39]____ .
A. Good idea!

Do you like to do any of these activities in your free time? Which ones?

What games are popular in your country? Describe how to play one.

МЕСТА РАЗВЛЕЧЕНИЙ

музей	**1**	museum	распродажа	**9**	yard sale
галерея	**2**	art gallery	вещей		
концерт	**3**	concert	на дому		
пьеса	**4**	play	толкучка/	**10**	swap meet/
парк аттракционов	**5**	amusement park	блошиный		flea market
историческое место	**6**	historic site	рынок		
заповедник/	**7**	national park	парк	**11**	park
национальный парк			пляж	**12**	beach
фестиваль рукоделия	**8**	craft fair	горы	**13**	mountains

аквариум	**14**	aquarium
ботанический сад	**15**	botanical gardens
планетарий	**16**	planetarium
зоопарк	**17**	zoo
кино	**18**	movies
ярмарка с	**19**	carnival
аттракционами		
ярмарка с	**20**	fair
аттракционами		

A. What do you want to do today?

B. Let's go to { a/an ___[1–9]___ .
           the ___[10–20]___ .

A. What did you do over the weekend?

B. I went to { a/an ___[1–9]___ .
        the ___[10–20]___ .

A. What are you going to do on your day off?

B. I'm going to go to { a/an ___[1–9]___ .
               the ___[10–20]___ .

What are some of your favorite places to go? Where are they? What do you do there?

велосипедная дорожка	**1**	bicycle path/ bike path/ bikeway	дорожка для бега	**8**	jogging path	детская площадка	**16**	playground
			скамейка	**9**	bench	стенка для лазанья	**17**	climbing wall
пруд с утками	**2**	duck pond	теннисный корт	**10**	tennis court	качели	**18**	swings
место для пикника	**3**	picnic area	бейсбольная площадка	**11**	ballfield	паутинка	**19**	climber
урна	**4**	trash can	фонтан	**12**	fountain	горка	**20**	slide
гриль	**5**	grill	стоянка велосипедов	**13**	bike rack	качели	**21**	seesaw
стол для пикника	**6**	picnic table	карусель	**14**	merry-go-round/ carousel	песочница	**22**	sandbox
фонтан с питьевой водой	**7**	water fountain	наклонная плоскость для скейтборда	**15**	skateboard ramp	песок	**23**	sand

[1–22]

A. Excuse me. Does this park have (a) _____?

B. Yes. Right over there.

[17–23]

A. { Be careful on the ___[17–21]___ !
    { Be careful in the ___[22, 23]___ !

B. I will, Dad/Mom.

Describe a park and playground you are familiar with.

спасатель	**1**	lifeguard		шезлонг/	**10**	beach chair		камень	**20**	rock
вышка спасателей	**2**	lifeguard stand		пляжное кресло				изотермический	**21**	cooler
спасательный круг	**3**	life preserver		пляжный зонт	**11**	beach umbrella		контейнер		
пляжный киоск	**4**	snack bar/		песочный замок	**12**	sand castle		пляжная шляпа	**22**	sun hat
		refreshment		доска для	**13**	boogie		крем для загара	**23**	sunscreen/
		stand		буги-сёрфинга		board				sunblock/
продавец на пляже	**5**	vendor		загорающий	**14**	sunbather				suntan lotion
пловец	**6**	swimmer		солнечные очки	**15**	sunglasses		пляжное	**24**	(beach)
волна	**7**	wave		пляжное полотенце	**16**	(beach) towel		покрывало		blanket
сёрфингист	**8**	surfer		надувной мяч	**17**	beach ball		лопатка	**25**	shovel
летучий змей	**9**	kite		доска для сёрфинга	**18**	surfboard		ведёрко	**26**	pail
				ракушка	**19**	seashell/shell				

[1–26]
A. What a nice beach!
B. It is. Look at all the _____s!

[9–11, 13, 15–18, 21–26]
A. Are you ready for the beach?
B. Almost. I just have to get my _____.

Do you like to go to the beach? Describe your favorite beach. What do you take when you go there?

ОТДЫХ НА ПРИРОДЕ

поход	**A**	**camping**
палатка	**1**	tent
спальный мешок	**2**	sleeping bag
колышки	**3**	tent stakes
фонарь	**4**	lantern
топорик	**5**	hatchet
походная плитка	**6**	camping stove
перочинный ножик	**7**	Swiss army knife
спрэй от насекомых	**8**	insect repellent
спички	**9**	matches

поход	**B**	**hiking**
рюкзак	**10**	backpack
фляжка	**11**	canteen
компас	**12**	compass
карта пути	**13**	trail map
портативный навигатор	**14**	GPS device
походные ботинки	**15**	hiking boots

скалолазание	**C**	**rock climbing/ technical climbing**
страховка	**16**	harness
верёвка	**17**	rope

велопоход	**D**	**mountain biking**
горный велосипед	**18**	mountain bike
велосипедный шлем	**19**	(bike) helmet

пикник	**E**	**picnic**
покрывало для пикника	**20**	(picnic) blanket
термос	**21**	thermos
корзина для пикника	**22**	picnic basket

A. Let's go ___[A–E]___ * this weekend.
B. Good idea! We haven't gone ___[A–E]___ * in a long time.

*With E, say: on a picnic.

A. Did you bring
 { the ___[1–9, 11–14, 16, 17, 20–22]___ ?
 { your ___[10, 15, 18, 19]___ ?
B. Yes, I did.
A. Oh, good.

Have you ever gone camping, hiking, rock climbing, or mountain biking? Tell about it: What did you do? Where? What equipment did you use?

Do you like to go on picnics? Where?
What picnic supplies and food do you take with you?

ИНДИВИДУАЛЬНЫЕ ВИДЫ СПОРТА И ОТДЫХА

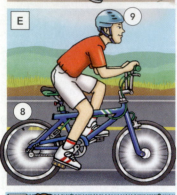

бег трусцой	**A jogging**		катание на лошади	**H horseback riding**
спортивный костюм	**1** jogging suit		седло	**14** saddle
кроссовки	**2** jogging shoes		вожжи	**15** reins
			стремя	**16** stirrups
бег	**B running**			
спортивные шорты	**3** running shorts		теннис	**I tennis**
кроссовки для бега	**4** running shoes		теннисная ракетка	**17** tennis racket
			теннисный мяч	**18** tennis ball
ходьба	**C walking**		теннисные шорты	**19** tennis shorts
кроссовки	**5** walking shoes			
			бадминтон	**J badminton**
катание на роликах	**D inline skating/rollerblading**		ракетка бадминтона	**20** badminton racket
ролики	**6** inline skates/rollerblades		воланчик	**21** birdie/shuttlecock
защита для коленей	**7** knee pads			
			ракетбол	**K racquetball**
катание на велосипеде	**E cycling/biking**		защитные очки	**22** safety goggles
велосипед	**8** bicycle/bike		мяч для ракетбола	**23** racquetball
велосипедный шлем	**9** (bicycle/bike) helmet		ракетка	**24** racquet
катание на скейтборде	**F skateboarding**		настольный теннис/	**L table tennis/**
скейтборд	**10** skateboard		пинг понг	**ping pong**
защита для локтей	**11** elbow pads		ракетка	**25** paddle
			стол для пинг понга	**26** ping pong table
боулинг	**G bowling**		сетка	**27** net
шар для боулинга	**12** bowling ball		мячик для пинг понга	**28** ping pong ball
ботинки для боулинга	**13** bowling shoes			

гольф	**M**	**golf**	
клюшки для гольфа	**29**	golf clubs	
мячик для гольфа	**30**	golf ball	
фрисби	**N**	**Frisbee**	
фрисби/ летающая тарелка	**31**	Frisbee/ flying disc	
бильярд	**O**	**billiards/pool**	
бильярдный стол	**32**	pool table	
кий	**33**	pool stick	
бильярдные шары	**34**	billiard balls	
боевые искусства	**P**	**martial arts**	
чёрный пояс	**35**	black belt	

гимнастика	**Q**	**gymnastics**
лошадь	**36**	horse
брусья	**37**	parallel bars
мат	**38**	mat
гимнастическое бревно	**39**	balance beam
батут	**40**	trampoline
тяжёлая атлетика	**R**	**weightlifting**
гантели	**41**	barbell
штанга	**42**	weights
стрельба из лука	**S**	**archery**
лук и стрела	**43**	bow and arrow
цель	**44**	target

бокс	**T**	**box**
боксёрские перчатки	**45**	boxing gloves
шорты для бокса	**46**	(boxing) trunks
борьба	**U**	**wrestle**
форма для борьбы	**47**	wrestling uniform
мат для борьбы	**48**	(wrestling) mat
занятия на тренажёрах	**V**	**work out/exercise**
беговая дорожка	**49**	treadmill
гребной тренажёр	**50**	rowing machine
велотренажёр	**51**	exercise bike
силовой тренажёр	**52**	universal/ exercise equipment

[A–V]

A. What do you like to do in your free time?

B.
- I like to go ___[A–H]___ .
- I like to play ___[I–O]___ .
- I like to do ___[P–S]___ .
- I like to ___[T–V]___ .

[1–52]

A. I really like this/these new _____ .

B. It's/They're very nice.

Do you do any of these activities? Which ones? Which are popular in your country?

КОМАНДНЫЕ ВИДЫ СПОРТА

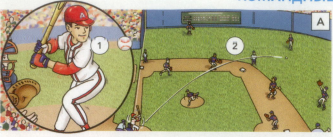

бейсбол	**A baseball**
игрок бейсбола	**1** baseball player
бейсбольная площадка	**2** baseball field/ballfield
софтбол	**B softball**
игрок софтбола	**3** softball player
площадка для софтбола	**4** ballfield
американский футбол	**C football**
игрок американского футбола	**5** football player

футбольное поле	**6** football field
лакросс	**D lacrosse**
игрок лакросса	**7** lacrosse player
площадка для лакросса	**8** lacrosse field
хоккей	**E (ice) hockey**
хоккеист	**9** hockey player
хоккейная площадка/каток	**10** hockey rink

баскетбол	**F basketball**
баскетболист	**11** basketball player
баскетбольная площадка	**12** basketball court
волейбол	**G volleyball**
волейболист	**13** volleyball player
волейбольная площадка	**14** volleyball court
футбол	**H soccer**
футболист	**15** soccer player
футбольное поле	**16** soccer field

[A–H]
A. Do you like to play **baseball**?
B. Yes. **Baseball** is one of my favorite sports.

A. ....plays __[A–H]__ very well.
B. You're right. I think he's/she's one of the best _____s* on the team.

*Use 1, 3, 5, 7, 9, 11, 13, 15.

A. Now listen, team! I want all of you to go out on that _____† and play the best game of __[A–H]__ you've ever played!
B. All right, Coach!

† Use 2, 4, 6, 8, 10, 12, 14, 16.

Which sports in this lesson do you like to play? Which do you like to watch?

What are your favorite teams?

Name some famous players of these sports.

СПОРТИВНОЕ ОБОРУДОВАНИЕ

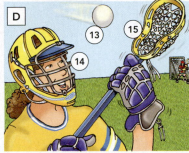

бейсбол	**A**	**baseball**
бейсбольный мяч	**1**	baseball
бита	**2**	bat
бейсбольный шлем	**3**	batting helmet
бейсбольная форма	**4**	(baseball) uniform
маска-шлем ловителя мяча	**5**	catcher's mask
бейсбольная перчатка	**6**	(baseball) glove
рукавица ловителя мяча	**7**	catcher's mitt
софтбол	**B**	**softball**
мяч для софтбола	**8**	softball
перчатка для софтбола	**9**	softball glove
американский футбол	**C**	**football**
мяч для американского футбола	**10**	football
шлем для американского футбола	**11**	football helmet
подплечники защиты плеча	**12**	shoulder pads

лакросс	**D**	**lacrosse**
мяч для лакросса	**13**	lacrosse ball
защитная маска	**14**	face guard
клюшка для лакросса	**15**	lacrosse stick
хоккей	**E**	**(ice) hockey**
шайба	**16**	hockey puck
хоккейная клюшка	**17**	hockey stick
маска-шлем вратаря	**18**	hockey mask
перчатки для хоккея	**19**	hockey glove
хоккейные коньки	**20**	hockey skates

баскетбол	**F**	**basketball**
баскетбольный мяч	**21**	basketball
баскетбольный щит	**22**	backboard
корзина	**23**	basketball hoop
волейбол	**G**	**volleyball**
волейбольный мяч	**24**	volleyball
волейбольная сетка	**25**	volleyball net
футбол	**H**	**soccer**
футбольный мяч	**26**	soccer ball
защита голени	**27**	shinguards

[1–27]
A. I can't find my **baseball**!
B. Look in the closet.*

*closet, basement, garage

[In a store]
A. Excuse me. I'm looking for (a) __[1–27]__ .
B. All our __[A–H]__ equipment is over there.
A. Thanks.

[At home]
A. I'm going to play __[A–H]__ after school today.
B. Don't forget your __[1–21, 24, 26, 27]__ !

Which sports in this lesson are popular in your country? Which sports do students play in high school?

катание на лыжах	**A**	**(downhill) skiing**
горные лыжи	1	skis
лыжные ботинки	2	ski boots
крепления	3	bindings
лыжные палки	4	(ski) poles
катание на лыжах	**B**	**cross-country skiing**
лыжи	5	cross-country skis
катание на коньках	**C**	**(ice) skating**
коньки	6	(ice) skates
лезвие	7	blade
насадка на лезвие	8	skate guard
фигурное катание	**D**	**figure skating**
фигурные коньки	9	figure skates

катание на сноуборде	**E**	**snowboarding**
доска для сноуборда	10	snowboard
катание на санках	**F**	**sledding**
санки	11	sled
поддон для катания/ поддон	12	sledding dish/ saucer
катание на бобслее/ салазках	**G**	**bobsledding**
бобслей/салазки	13	bobsled
катание на снегоходе	**H**	**snowmobiling**
снегоход	14	snowmobile

[A–H]
A. What's your favorite winter sport?
B. **Skiing**.

[A–H]

[At work or at school on Friday]
A. What are you going to do this weekend?
B. I'm going to go _____ .

[1–14]

[On the telephone]
A. Hello. *Sally's* Sporting Goods.
B. Hello. Do you sell _____(s)?
A. Yes, we do. / No, we don't.

Have you ever done any of these activities? Which ones?

Have you ever watched the Winter Olympics? Which event do you think is the most exciting? the most dangerous?

ВОДНЫЙ СПОРТ И ОТДЫХ

кораблевождение	**A sailing**		погружение с аквалангом	**H scuba diving**
парусное судно	**1** sailboat		гидрокостюм	**17** wet suit
спасательный жилет	**2** life jacket/life vest		баллон с воздухом	**18** (air) tank
			маска акваланиста	**19** (diving) mask
плавать на каноэ	**B canoeing**			
каноэ	**3** canoe		катание на волнах/	**I surfing**
вёсла	**4** paddles		сёрфинг	
			доска для сёрфинга	**20** surfboard
кататься на лодке	**C rowing**			
лодка	**5** rowboat		катание на паруснике/	**J windsurfing**
вёсла	**6** oars		виндсёрфинг	
			парусная доска/	**21** sailboard
каякинг	**D kayaking**		виндсёрфер	
каяк	**7** kayak		парус	**22** sail
вёсла	**8** paddles			
			катание на	**K waterskiing**
рафтинг	**E (white-water) rafting**		водных лыжах	
рафт	**9** raft		водные лыжи	**23** water skis
спасательный жилет	**10** life jacket/life vest		трос	**24** towrope
плавание	**F swimming**		рыбалка	**L fishing**
купальник	**11** swimsuit/bathing suit		удочка	**25** (fishing) rod/ pole
очки	**12** goggles		катушка	**26** reel
резиновая шапочка	**13** bathing cap		рыболовная леска	**27** (fishing) line
			рыболовная сеть	**28** (fishing) net
подводное плавание	**G snorkeling**		приманка	**29** bait
маска	**14** mask			
дыхательная трубка	**15** snorkel			
ласты	**16** fins			

[A–L]
A. Would you like to go **sailing** tomorrow?
B. Sure. I'd love to.

A. Have you ever gone __[A–L]__?
B. Yes, I have. / No, I haven't.

A. Do you have everything you need to go __[A–L]__?
B. Yes. I have my __[1–29]__ (and my __[1–29]__).
A. Have a good time!

Which sports in this lesson have you tried? Which sports would you like to try?

Are any of these sports popular in your country? Which ones?

СПОРТИВНЫЕ ЗАНЯТИЯ

ударять	**1**	hit	делать растяжку	**11**	stretch	
подавать	**2**	pitch	сгибаться	**12**	bend	
кидать	**3**	throw	ходить	**13**	walk	
ловить	**4**	catch	бегать	**14**	run	
передавать	**5**	pass	подпрыгивать	**15**	hop	
пинать	**6**	kick	скакать	**16**	skip	
подавать	**7**	serve	прыгать	**17**	jump	
отбивать	**8**	bounce	тянуться	**18**	reach	
вести (мяч)	**9**	dribble	размахивать	**19**	swing	
бросать	**10**	shoot	поднимать	**20**	lift	

плавать	**21**	swim
нырять	**22**	dive
стрелять	**23**	shoot
отжимание	**24**	push-up
пресс	**25**	sit-up
приседание	**26**	deep knee bend
прыжки на месте	**27**	jumping jack
кувыркание	**28**	somersault
"колесо"	**29**	cartwheel
стояние на руках	**30**	handstand

[1–10]
A. _____ the ball!
B. Okay, Coach!

[11–23]
A. Now _____!
B. Like this?
A. Yes.

[24–30]
A. Okay, everybody. I want you to do twenty _____s!
B. Twenty _____s?!
A. That's right.

Do you exercise regularly?
Which exercises do you do?

Be an exercise instructor! Lead your friends in an exercise
routine using the actions in this lesson.

РАЗВЛЕЧЕНИЯ

пьеса/спектакль	**A**	**play**
театральный зал	**1**	theater
актёр	**2**	actor
актриса	**3**	actress

	B	**concert**
концерт		
концертный зал	**4**	concert hall
оркестр	**5**	orchestra
музыкант	**6**	musician
дирижёр	**7**	conductor
группа	**8**	band

опера	**C**	**opera**
оперная певица	**9**	opera singer

балет	**D**	**ballet**
артист балета	**10**	ballet dancer
балерина	**11**	ballerina

музыкальный клуб	**E**	**music club**
певица	**12**	singer

кино	**F**	**movies**
кинотеатр	**13**	(movie) theater
экран	**14**	(movie) screen
актриса	**15**	actress
актёр	**16**	actor

клуб сатиры и юмора	**G**	**comedy club**
сатирик	**17**	comedian

[A–G]
A. What are you doing this evening?
B. I'm going to {
a _____[A, B, E, G]_____.
the _____[C, D, F]_____.
}

[1–17]
A. What a magnificent _____!
B. I agree.

What kinds of entertainment in this lesson do you like?
What kinds of entertainment are popular in your country?

Who are some of your favorite actors? actresses?
musicians? singers? comedians?

ВИДЫ РАЗВЛЕЧЕНИЙ

A

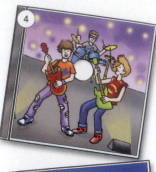

B

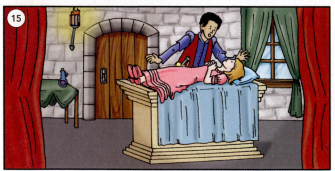

музыка	**A**	**music**	рэп музыка	**6**	rap music	пьесы	**B**	**plays**
классическая музыка	**1**	classical music	христианская музыка	**7**	gospel music	драма	**13**	drama
поп музыка	**2**	popular music	джаз	**8**	jazz	комедия	**14**	comedy
музыка кантри	**3**	country music	блюз	**9**	blues	трагедия	**15**	tragedy
рок музыка	**4**	rock music	кантри	**10**	bluegrass	музыкальная	**16**	musical
народная музыка	**5**	folk music	хип хоп	**11**	hip hop	комедия		(comedy)
			регги	**12**	reggae			

кино/фильмы	**C**	**movies/films**
драма	**17**	drama
комедия	**18**	comedy
вестерн	**19**	western
детектив	**20**	mystery
мюзикл	**21**	musical
мультфильм	**22**	cartoon
документальный фильм	**23**	documentary
приключенческий фильм	**24**	action movie/ adventure movie

военный фильм	**25**	war movie
фильм ужасов	**26**	horror movie
фантастический фильм	**27**	science fiction movie
зарубежное кино	**28**	foreign film

телепередачи	**D**	**TV programs**
драма	**29**	drama
комическая ситуация/ комедия	**30**	(situation) comedy/ sitcom
ток шоу	**31**	talk show
телеигра/ телевикторина	**32**	game show/ quiz show

шоу реальности	**33**	reality show
мыльная опера	**34**	soap opera
мультфильм	**35**	cartoon
детская передача	**36**	children's program
новости	**37**	news program
спортивная передача	**38**	sports program
передача о природе	**39**	nature program
телемагазин	**40**	shopping program

A. What kind of ___[A–D]___ do you like?
B. { I like ___[1–12]___ .
{ I like ___[13–40]___ s.

What's your favorite type of music?
Who is your favorite singer? musician?
musical group?

What kind of movies do you like?
Who are your favorite movie stars?
What are the titles of your favorite movies?

What kind of TV programs do you like?
What are your favorite shows?

МУЗЫКАЛЬНЫЕ ИНСТРУМЕНТЫ

Струнные Инструменты	Strings		Деревянные Духовые Инструменты	Woodwinds		Ударные Инструменты	Percussion
скрипка	**1**	violin	малая флейта/пикколо	**9**	piccolo	барабаны	**20** drums
альт	**2**	viola	флейта	**10**	flute	тарелки	**a** cymbals
виолончель	**3**	cello	кларнет	**11**	clarinet	бубен	**21** tambourine
контрабас	**4**	bass	гобой	**12**	oboe	ксилофон	**22** xylophone
акустическая гитара	**5**	(acoustic) guitar	блок-флейта	**13**	recorder	**Клавишные Инструменты**	**Keyboard Instruments**
электрогитара	**6**	electric guitar	саксофон	**14**	saxophone	рояль/пианино	**23** piano
банджо	**7**	banjo	фагот	**15**	bassoon	синтезатор	**24** electric keyboard
арфа	**8**	harp	**Медные Духовые Инструменты**	**Brass**		орган	**25** organ
			труба	**16**	trumpet	**Прочие Инструменты**	**Other Instruments**
			тромбон	**17**	trombone	аккордеон	**26** accordion
			валторна	**18**	French horn	губная гармошка	**27** harmonica
			туба музыкальная	**19**	tuba		

A. Do you play a musical instrument?
B. Yes. I play the **violin**.

A. You play the **trumpet** very well.
B. Thank you.

A. What's that noise?!
B. That's my son/daughter practicing the **drums**.

Do you play a musical instrument? Which one?

Which instruments are usually in an orchestra? a marching band? a rock group?

Name and describe typical musical instruments in your country.

ФЕРМА И СЕЛЬСКОХОЗЯЙСТВЕННЫЕ ЖИВОТНЫЕ

дом на ферме	**1**	farmhouse	петух	**14**	rooster	корова	**26**	cow
фермер	**2**	farmer	свинарник	**15**	pig pen	овца	**27**	sheep
огород	**3**	(vegetable) garden	свинья	**16**	pig	фруктовый сад	**28**	orchard
огородное пугало	**4**	scarecrow	курятник	**17**	chicken coop	фруктовое дерево	**29**	fruit tree
сено	**5**	hay	курица	**18**	chicken	фермерский рабочий	**30**	farm worker
наёмный рабочий	**6**	hired hand	насест	**19**	hen house	люцерна	**31**	alfalfa
амбар	**7**	barn	курица	**20**	hen	кукуруза	**32**	corn
конюшня/стойло	**8**	stable	посев	**21**	crop	хлопок	**33**	cotton
лошадь	**9**	horse	система поливки участка	**22**	irrigation system	рис	**34**	rice
скотный двор	**10**	barnyard	трактор	**23**	tractor	соя	**35**	soybeans
индюк	**11**	turkey	поле	**24**	field	пшеница	**36**	wheat
коза	**12**	goat	пастбище	**25**	pasture			
ягнёнок	**13**	lamb						

[1–30]
A. Where's the _____?
B. In / Next to the _____.

A. The _[9, 11–14, 16, 18, 20, 26]_ s / _[27]_ are loose again!
B. Oh, no! Where are they?
A. They're in the _[1, 3, 7, 8, 10, 15, 17, 19, 24, 25, 28]_.

[31–36]
A. Do you grow _____ on your farm?
B. No. We grow _____.

Tell about farms in your country. What crops and animals are common on these farms?

ЖИВОТНЫЕ И ДОМАШНИЕ ЖИВОТНЫЕ

лось	**1**	moose	заяц	**13**	rabbit
рог	**a**	antler	бобёр	**14**	beaver
белый медведь	**2**	polar bear	енот	**15**	raccoon
олень	**3**	deer	опоссум	**16**	possum/
копыто-копыта	**a**	hoof-hooves			opossum
волк-волки	**4**	wolf-wolves	лошадь	**17**	horse
шкура/мех	**a**	coat/fur	хвост	**a**	tail
барибал/чёрный	**5**	(black) bear	пони	**18**	pony
медведь			осёл	**19**	donkey
коготь	**a**	claw	броненосец	**20**	armadillo
пума	**6**	mountain lion	летучая мышь	**21**	bat
медведь гризли	**7**	(grizzly) bear	червяк	**22**	worm
буйвол/бизон	**8**	buffalo/bison	слизняк	**23**	slug
койот	**9**	coyote	обезьяна	**24**	monkey
лиса	**10**	fox	муравьед	**25**	anteater
скунс	**11**	skunk	лама	**26**	llama
дикобраз	**12**	porcupine	ягуар	**27**	jaguar
иголка	**a**	quill	пятна	**a**	spots

мышь-мыши	**28**	mouse-mice
крыса	**29**	rat
бурундук	**30**	chipmunk
белка	**31**	squirrel
суслик	**32**	gopher
луговая собачка	**33**	prairie dog
кот	**34**	cat
усы	**a**	whiskers
котёнок	**35**	kitten
собака	**36**	dog
щенок	**37**	puppy
хомяк	**38**	hamster
карликовая песчанка	**39**	gerbil
морская свинка	**40**	guinea pig
золотая рыбка	**41**	goldfish
канарейка	**42**	canary
волнистый попугай	**43**	parakeet

антилопа	**44**	antelope		тигр	**51**	tiger		лев	**55**	lion		горилла	**61**	gorilla
бабуин	**45**	baboon		лапа		**a** paw		грива		**a** mane		кенгуру	**62**	kangaroo
носорог	**46**	rhinoceros		верблюд	**52**	camel		жираф	**56**	giraffe		сумка		**a** pouch
рог		**a** horn		горб		**a** hump		зебра	**57**	zebra		коала	**63**	koala (bear)
панда	**47**	panda		слон	**53**	elephant		полоски		**a** stripes		утконос	**64**	platypus
орангутанг	**48**	orangutan		бивень		**a** tusk		шимпанзе	**58**	chimpanzee
пантера	**49**	panther		хобот		**b** trunk		бегемот	**59**	hippopotamus
гиббон	**50**	gibbon		гиена	**54**	hyena		леопард	**60**	leopard

[1–33, 44–64]
A. Look at that _____!
B. Wow! That's the biggest _____ I've ever seen!

[34–43]
A. Do you have a pet?
B. Yes. I have a _____.
A. What's your _____'s name?
B. ....

What animals are there where you live?

Is there a zoo near where you live? What animals does it have?

What are some common pets in your country?

If you could be an animal, which animal would you like to be? Why?

Does your culture have any popular folk tales or children's stories about animals? Tell a story you know.

ПТИЦЫ И НАСЕКОМЫЕ

Птицы		Birds
малиновка	**1**	robin
гнездо	**a**	nest
яйцо	**b**	egg
голубая сойка	**2**	blue jay
крыло	**a**	wing
хвост	**b**	tail
перо	**c**	feather
кардинал	**3**	cardinal
ворона	**4**	crow
чайка	**5**	seagull
дятел	**6**	woodpecker
клюв	**a**	beak
голубь	**7**	pigeon
сова	**8**	owl
сокол	**9**	hawk

орёл	**10**	eagle
коготь	**a**	claw
лебедь	**11**	swan
колибри	**12**	hummingbird
утка	**13**	duck
клюв	**a**	bill
воробей	**14**	sparrow
гусь-гуси	**15**	goose-geese
пингвин	**16**	penguin
фламинго	**17**	flamingo
журавль	**18**	crane
аист	**19**	stork
пеликан	**20**	pelican
павлин	**21**	peacock
попугай	**22**	parrot
страус	**23**	ostrich

Насекомые		Insects
муха	**24**	fly
божья коровка	**25**	ladybug
светлячок	**26**	firefly/ lightning bug
мотылёк	**27**	moth
гусеница	**28**	caterpillar
кокон	**a**	cocoon
бабочка	**29**	butterfly
клещ	**30**	tick
комар	**31**	mosquito
стрекоза	**32**	dragonfly
паук	**33**	spider
паутина	**a**	web

богомол	**34**	praying mantis
оса	**35**	wasp
пчела	**36**	bee
улей	**a**	beehive
кузнечик	**37**	grasshopper
жук	**38**	beetle
скорпион	**39**	scorpion
сороконожка	**40**	centipede
сверчок	**41**	cricket

[1–41]
A. Is that a/an _____ ?
B. No. I think it's a/an _____ .

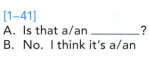

[24–41]
A. Hold still! There's a _____ on your shirt!
B. Oh! Can you get it off me?
A. There! It's gone!

What birds and insects are there where you live?

Does your culture have any popular folk tales or children's stories about birds or insects? Tell a story you know.

РЫБЫ, МОРСКИЕ ЖИВОТНЫЕ И РЕПТИЛИИ

Рыбы		Fish
форель	**1**	trout
плавник	**a**	fin
жабры	**b**	gill
чешуя	**c**	scales
камбала	**2**	flounder
тунец	**3**	tuna
рыба меч	**4**	swordfish
окунь	**5**	bass
акула	**6**	shark
угорь	**7**	eel
треска	**8**	cod
скат	**9**	ray/stingray
морской конёк	**10**	sea horse

Морские Животные		Sea Animals
кит	**11**	whale
дельфин	**12**	dolphin
морская свинья	**13**	porpoise
медуза	**14**	jellyfish
осьминог	**15**	octopus
щупальце	**a**	tentacle
морской котик	**16**	seal
морской лев	**17**	sea lion
выдра	**18**	otter
морж	**19**	walrus
бивень	**a**	tusk
краб	**20**	crab
кальмар	**21**	squid
улитка	**22**	snail
морская звезда	**23**	starfish
морской ёж	**24**	sea urchin
актиния	**25**	sea anemone

Амфибии и Рептилии		Amphibians and Reptiles
сухопутная черепаха	**26**	tortoise
панцирь	**a**	shell
водная черепаха	**27**	turtle
аллигатор	**28**	alligator
крокодил	**29**	crocodile
ящерица	**30**	lizard
игуана	**31**	iguana
лягушка	**32**	frog
тритон	**33**	newt
саламандра	**34**	salamander
жаба	**35**	toad
змея	**36**	snake
гремучая змея	**37**	rattlesnake
удав	**38**	boa constrictor
кобра	**39**	cobra

[1–39]
A. Is that a/an _____?
B. No. I think it's a/an _____.

[26–39]
A. Are there any _____s around here?
B. No. But there are lots of _____!

What fish, sea animals, and reptiles can be found in your country? Which ones are endangered and need to be protected? Why?

In your opinion, which ones are the most interesting? the most beautiful? the most dangerous?

ДЕРЕВЬЯ, РАСТЕНИЯ И ЦВЕТЫ

дерево	**1**	tree	кизил	**11**	dogwood
лист-листья	**2**	leaf-leaves	остролист	**12**	holly
веточка	**3**	twig	магнолия	**13**	magnolia
ветка	**4**	branch	вяз	**14**	elm
ветвь	**5**	limb	вишня	**15**	cherry
ствол	**6**	trunk	пальма	**16**	palm
кора	**7**	bark	берёза	**17**	birch
корень	**8**	root	клён	**18**	maple
иголка	**9**	needle	дуб	**19**	oak
шишка	**10**	pine cone	сосна	**20**	pine

красное дерево	**21**	redwood	растение	**28**	plant
ива	**22**	(weeping) willow	кактус-кактусы	**29**	cactus-cacti
куст	**23**	bush	вьющийся стебель	**30**	vine
куст	**24**	holly	ядовитый плющ	**31**	poison ivy
остролиста			ядовитый сумах	**32**	poison sumac
ягоды	**25**	berries	ядовитый дуб	**33**	poison oak
кустарник	**26**	shrub			
папоротник	**27**	fern			

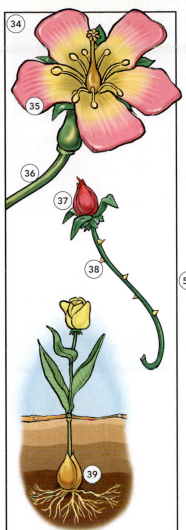

цветок	**34** flower	ноготки, бархатцы	**43** marigold	подсолнух	**52** sunflower
лепесток	**35** petal	гвоздика	**44** carnation	крокус	**53** crocus
стебель	**36** stem	гардения	**45** gardenia	тюльпан	**54** tulip
почка	**37** bud	лилия	**46** lily	герань	**55** geranium
шип	**38** thorn	ирис	**47** iris	фиалка	**56** violet
луковица	**39** bulb	анютины глазки	**48** pansy	пуансеттия	**57** poinsettia
хризантема	**40** chrysanthemum	петуния	**49** petunia	жасмин	**58** jasmine
жёлтый нарцисс	**41** daffodil	орхидея	**50** orchid	гибискус	**59** hibiscus
ромашка	**42** daisy	роза	**51** rose		

[11–22]
A. What kind of tree is that?
B. I think it's a/an _____ tree.

[31–33]
A. Watch out for the _____ over there!
B. Oh. Thanks for the warning.

[40–57]
A. Look at all the _____s!*
B. They're beautiful!

*With 58 and 59, use: Look at all the ___!

Describe your favorite tree and your favorite flower.

What kinds of trees and flowers grow where you live?

In your country, what flowers do you see at weddings? at funerals? during holidays? in hospital rooms? Tell which flowers people use for different occasions.

ЭНЕРГИЯ, ЭКОНОМИЯ ПРИРОДНЫХ РЕСУРСОВ И ОКРУЖАЮЩАЯ СРЕДА

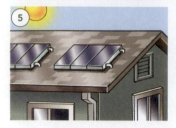

Источники Энергии	Sources of Energy	Экономия Природных Ресурсов	Conservation	Проблемы Экологии	Environmental Problems
нефть	**1** oil/petroleum	переработать	**9** recycle	загрязнения воздуха	**13** air pollution
природный газ	**2** (natural) gas	экономить энергию	**10** save energy/ conserve energy	загрязнение воды	**14** water pollution
уголь	**3** coal			выброс опасных веществ/	**15** hazardous waste/ toxic waste
ядерная энергия	**4** nuclear energy	экономить воду	**11** save water/ conserve water	выброс токсичных веществ	
солнечная энергия	**5** solar energy				
гидроэлектрическая энергия	**6** hydroelectric power	совместно использовать машину	**12** carpool	кислотный дождь	**16** acid rain
ветер	**7** wind			радиация	**17** radiation
геотермическая энергия	**8** geothermal energy			глобальное потепление	**18** global warming

[1–8]
A. In my opinion, _____ will be our best source of energy in the future.
B. I disagree. I think our best source of energy will be _____.

[9–12]
A. Do you _____?
B. Yes. I'm very concerned about the environment.

[13–18]
A. Do you worry about the environment?
B. Yes. I'm very concerned about _____.

What kind of energy do you use to heat your home? to cook? In your opinion, which will be the best source of energy in the future?

Do you practice conservation? What do you do to help the environment?

In your opinion, what is the most serious environmental problem in the world today? Why?

СТИХИЙНЫЕ БЕДСТВИЯ

землетрясение	**1** earthquake	
ураган	**2** hurricane	
тайфун	**3** typhoon	
снежная буря/пурга	**4** blizzard	
смерч	**5** tornado	

наводнение	**6** flood
цунами	**7** tsunami
засуха	**8** drought
лесной пожар	**9** forest fire
блуждающий пожар	**10** wildfire

оползень	**11** landslide
грязевой оползень	**12** mudslide
лавина	**13** avalanche
извержение вулкана	**14** volcanic eruption

A. Did you hear about the _____ in ......(country)......?
B. Yes, I did. I saw it on the news.

Have you or someone you know ever experienced a natural disaster? Tell about it.

Which natural disasters sometimes happen where you live? How do people prepare for them?

FORMS OF IDENTIFICATION

ДОКУМЕНТЫ

1

2

3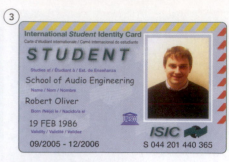

4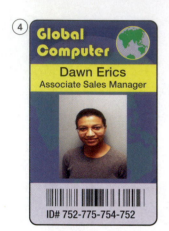

5

6

7

8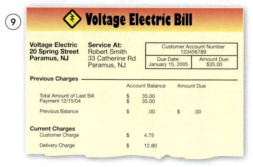

9

10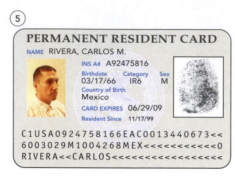

водительские права	**1**	driver's license	удостоверение	**5**	permanent resident card	доказательство места жительства	**9**	proof of residence
карточка социального обеспечения	**2**	social security card	паспорт	**6**	passport	свидетельство о рождении	**10**	birth certificate
студенческий билет	**3**	student I.D. card	виза	**7**	visa			
пропуск	**4**	employee I.D. badge	разрешение на работу	**8**	work permit			

A. May I see your _____?
B. Yes. Here you are.

A. Oh, no! I can't find my _____!
B. I'll help you look for it.
A. Thanks.

Which forms of identification do you have? When do you need to show them?

ПРАВИТЕЛЬСТВО США

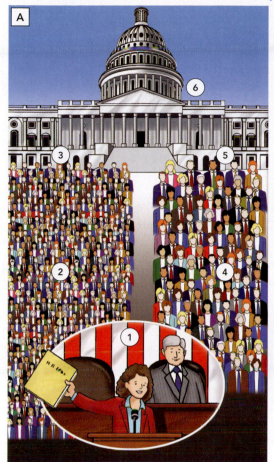

Законодательный Орган	**A legislative branch**	Исполнительный Орган	**B executive branch**	Судебный Орган	**C judicial branch**
создаёт законы	**1** makes the laws	приводит законы в исполнение	**7** enforces the laws	разъясняет законы	**12** explains the laws
представители	**2** representatives/ congressmen and congresswomen	президент	**8** president	судьи Верховного Суда	**13** Supreme Court justices
палата представителей	**3** house of representatives	вице президент	**9** vice-president	председатель Верховного Суда	**14** chief justice
сенаторы	**4** senators	кабинет министров/ правительство	**10** cabinet	Верховный Суд	**15** Supreme Court
сенат	**5** senate	Белый Дом	**11** White House	Здание Верховного Суда	**16** Supreme Court Building
Здание Конгресса	**6** Capitol Building				

A. Which branch of government __[1, 7, 12]__ ?
B. The __[A, B, C]__ .

A. Who works in the __[A, B, C]__ of the government?
B. The __[2, 4, 8–10, 13, 14]__ .

A. Where do/does the __[2, 4, 8–10, 13, 14]__ work?
B. In the __[6, 11, 16]__ .

A. In which branch of the government is the __[3, 5, 10, 15]__ ?
B. In the __[A, B, C]__ .

Compare the governments of different countries you are familiar with. What are the branches of government? Who works there? What do they do?

A 1
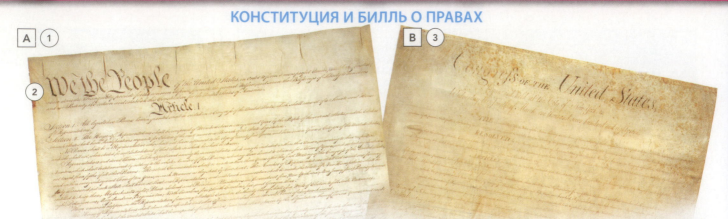
B 3

C 4

5

6

7

D 8 13th

9 15th

10 16th

11 19th

12 26th

Конституция	**A**	**The Constitution**
высшее право страны	**1**	"the supreme law of the land"
Вступление	**2**	the Preamble

| **Билль о Правах** | **B** | **The Bill of Rights** |
| первые десять поправок к Конституции | **3** | the first 10 amendments to the Constitution |

Первая Поправка к Конституции США	**C**	**The 1st Amendment**
свобода слова	**4**	freedom of speech
свобода печати	**5**	freedom of the press
свобода вероисповедания	**6**	freedom of religion
свобода собраний	**7**	freedom of assembly

Другие Поправки	**D**	**Other Amendments**
отменили рабство	**8**	ended slavery
дали право голосовать Афроамериканцам	**9**	gave African-Americans the right to vote
установили подоходные налоги	**10**	established income taxes
дали женщинам право голосовать	**11**	gave women the right to vote
дали право голосовать гражданам восемнадцати лет и старше	**12**	gave citizens eighteen years and older the right to vote

A. What is ___[A ,B]___?
B. ___[1 ,3]___.

A. Which amendment guarantees people ___[4–7]___?
B. The 1st Amendment.

A. Which amendment ___[8–12]___?
B. The _____ Amendment.

A. What did the _____ Amendment do?
B. It ___[8–12]___.

Describe how people in your community exercise their 1st Amendment rights. What are some examples of freedom of speech? the press? religion? assembly?

Do you have an idea for a new amendment? Tell about it and why you think it's important.

СОБЫТИЯ В ИСТОРИИ США

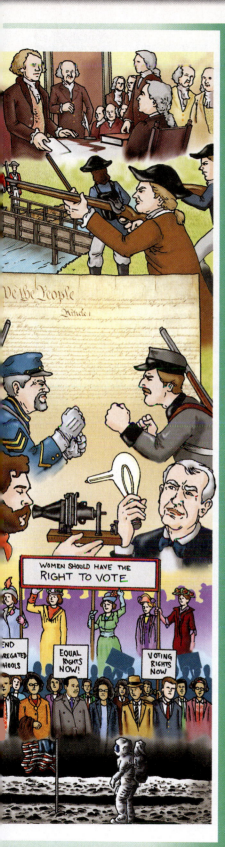

T I M E L I N E

1607	Colonists come to Jamestown, Virginia.
	Колонисты приходят в Джеймстаун, Вирджиния.
1620	Pilgrims come to the Plymouth Colony.
	Странники приходят в Плимутскую Колонию.
1775	The Revolutionary War begins.
	Начинается Война за Независимость Америки.
1776	The colonies declare their independence.
	Колонии провозглашают свою независимость.
1783	The Revolutionary War ends.
	Заканчивается Война за Независимость.
1787	Representatives write the United States Constitution.
	Представители палаты пишут Конституцию Америки.
1789	George Washington becomes the first president.
	Джордж Вашингтон становиться первым президентом.
1791	The Bill of Rights is added to the Constitution.
	Билль о Правах добавляется в Конституцию.
1861	The Civil War begins.
	Начинается Гражданская Война.
1863	President Lincoln signs the Emancipation Proclamation.
	Президент Линкольн подписывает Манифест об Освобождении Рабов.
1865	The Civil War ends.
	Заканчивается Гражданская Война.
1876	Alexander Graham Bell invents the telephone.
	Александер Грэм Белл изобретает телефон.
1879	Thomas Edison invents the lightbulb.
	Томас Эдисон изобретает электрическую лампочку.
1914	World War I (One) begins.
	Начинается Первая Мировая Война.
1918	World War I (One) ends.
	Заканчивается Первая Мировая Война.
1920	Women get the right to vote.
	Женщины получают право голосовать.
1929	The stock market crashes, and the Great Depression begins.
	Происходит обвал фондовой биржи. Начинается Великая Депрессия.
1939	World War II (Two) begins.
	Начинается Вторая Мировая Война.
1945	World War II (Two) ends.
	Заканчивается Вторая Мировая Война.
1950	The Korean War begins.
	Начинается Война в Корее.
1953	The Korean War ends.
	Заканчивается Война в Корее.
1954	The civil rights movement begins.
	Начинается движение за гражданские права.
1963	The March on Washington takes place.
	Идёт Марш на Вашингтон.
1964	The Vietnam War begins.
	Начинается Война во Вьетнаме.
1969	Astronaut Neil Armstrong lands on the moon.
	Астронавт Нил Армстронг совершает посадку на Луне.
1973	The Vietnam War ends.
	Заканчивается Война во Вьетнаме.
1991	The Persian Gulf War occurs.
	Происходит война в Персидском Заливе
2001	The United States is attacked by terrorists.
	Соединённые Штаты подвергаются нападению террористов.

A. What happened in ......(year)......?
B. ......(Event)...... ed.

A. When did ......(event)......?
B. In ......(year)...... .

In your opinion, which event in this lesson is the most important? Why?

Tell about important events in the history of your country.

ПРАЗДНИКИ

Новый Год	1	New Year's Day
День Мартина Лютера Кинга Младшего	2	Martin Luther King, Jr.* Day
День Святого Валентина	3	Valentine's Day
День Памяти Погибших на Войне	4	Memorial Day
День Независимости Америки	5	Independence Day/ the Fourth of July
Хэллоуин	6	Halloween

День Ветеранов Войны	7	Veterans Day
День Благодарения	8	Thanksgiving
Рождество	9	Christmas
Рамадан	10	Ramadan
Кванза	11	Kwanzaa
Ханука	12	Hanukkah

* Jr. = Junior

A. When is ___[1, 3, 5, 6, 7, 9]___?
B. It's on _____(date)_____.

A. When is __[2, 4, 8]__?
B. It's in _____(month)_____.

A. When does ____[10–12]____ begin this year?
B. It begins on _____(date)_____.

Which of these holidays do you celebrate? How?　　　　What holidays do people celebrate in your country?

ЗАКОНОДАТЕЛЬСТВО

You have the right to remain silent.

$10,000

Not Guilty!

Guilty!

5 years!

$100,000

быть арестованным	**A**	be arrested
сдавать данные в полицейском участке	**B**	be booked at the police station
нанять адвоката	**C**	hire a lawyer/ hire an attorney
присутствовать на суде	**D**	appear in court
предстать перед судом	**E**	stand* trial
быть оправданным	**F**	be acquitted
быть осуждённым	**G**	be convicted
быть приговорённым	**H**	be sentenced
садиться в тюрьму	**I**	go to jail/prison
быть освобождённым	**J**	be released
подозреваемый	**1**	suspect
полицейский	**2**	police officer

*stand-stood

наручники	**3**	handcuffs
"права Миранды"	**4**	Miranda rights
отпечатки пальцев	**5**	fingerprints
фото взятое в полиции	**6**	mug shot/ police photo
адвокат	**7**	lawyer/attorney
судья	**8**	judge
подсудимый	**9**	defendant
залог	**10**	bail
зал суда	**11**	courtroom
обвинитель	**12**	prosecuting attorney
свидетель	**13**	witness
протоколист суда	**14**	court reporter

защитник	**15**	defense attorney
свидетельские показания	**16**	evidence
судебный пристав	**17**	bailiff
присяжные	**18**	jury
вердикт/решение присяжных	**19**	verdict
невиновный	**20**	innocent/ not guilty
виновный	**21**	guilty
приговор	**22**	sentence
штраф	**23**	fine
тюремщик	**24**	prison guard
осуждённый/ заключённый	**25**	convict/prisoner/ inmate

[A–J]
A. Did you hear about _____(name)_____?
B. No, I didn't.
A. He/She _____ed.
B. Really? I didn't know that.

[A–J]
A. What happened in the last episode?
B. _____(name of character)_____ _____ed.

[1, 2, 7–9, 12–15, 17, 24, 25]
A. Are you the _____?
B. No. I'm the _____.

Tell about the legal system in your country. Describe what happens after a person is arrested.

Do you watch any crime shows on TV? Which ones? Tell about an episode you remember.

CITIZENSHIP
ГРАЖДАНСТВО

I hereby declare . . .

branches of government
legislative
executive
judicial

NO SWIMMING

U.S. Treasury

Права и Обязанности Граждан	Citizens' Rights and Responsibilities
голосовать	**1** vote
соблюдать законы	**2** obey laws
платить налоги	**3** pay taxes
быть присяжным на суде	**4** serve on a jury
быть частью общественной жизни	**5** be part of community life
следить за текущими новостями	**6** follow the news to know about current events
зарегистрироваться в Системе Воинской Повинности	**7** register with the Selective Service System*

* Все лица мужского пола проживающие на территории США должны зарегистрироваться на Воинскую Повинность.

Процесс Получения Гражданства	The Path to Citizenship
подавать заявление на гражданство	**8** apply for citizenship
узнавать о истории и правительстве Америки	**9** learn about U.S. government and history
сдавать экзамен на гражданство	**10** take a citizenship test
проходить собеседование на гражданство	**11** have a naturalization interview
присутствовать на церемонии получения гражданства	**12** attend a naturalization ceremony
давать Присягу на Верность	**13** recite the Oath of Allegiance

A. Can you name one responsibility of United States citizens?
B. Yes. Citizens should ____[1–7]____.

A. How is your citizenship application coming along?
B. Very well. I ____[8–11]____ed, and now I'm preparing to ____[9–13]____.
A. Good luck!

In your opinion, what are the most important rights and responsibilities of all people in their communities?

In your opinion, should non-citizens have all the same rights as citizens? Why or why not?

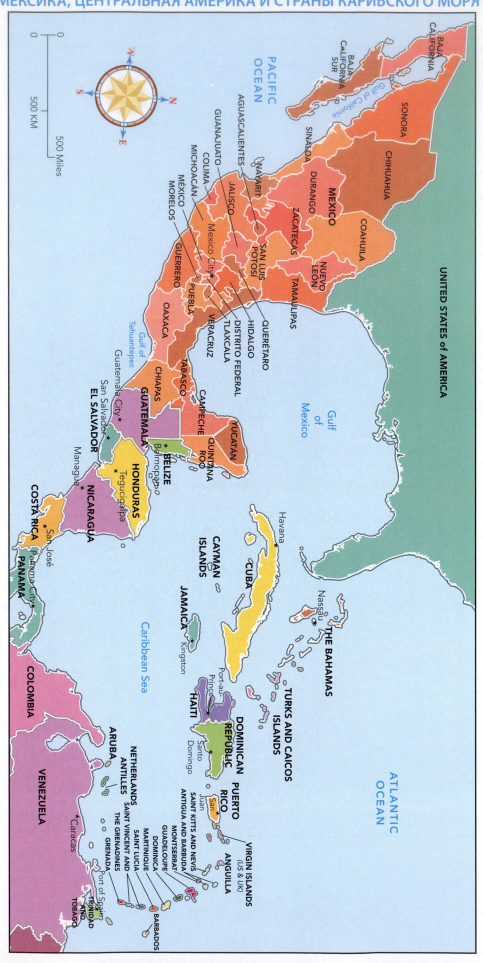

ЮЖНАЯ АМЕРИКА

Caribbean Sea

Barranquilla
Cartagena
Maracaibo
Valencia
Barquisimeto
Caracas

ATLANTIC
OCEAN

VENEZUELA

Georgetown

Medellín

GUYANA

Paramaribo
Cayenne

Bogotá

SURINAME

FRENCH
GUIANA

Cali

COLOMBIA

Equator
Quito
ECUADOR

Equator

Belém

Gulf of
Guayaquil

Guayaquil

Manaus

Fortaleza

Teresina

PERU

BRAZIL

Recife

Lima

Salvador

La Paz

Brasília

BOLIVIA

Goiânia

Sucre

Belo Horizonte

PARAGUAY

Rio de Janeiro

CHILE

Campinas
São Paulo

Asuncion

Curitiba

PACIFIC
OCEAN

ARGENTINA

Pôrto Alegre

Córdoba

Rosario

URUGUAY

Santiago

Buenos Aires

Montevideo

Gulf of San Matías

ATLANTIC
OCEAN

Gulf of
San Jorge

N

W   E

FALKLAND
ISLANDS

S

Strait of Magellan

Port Stanley

SOUTH GEORGIA
ISLAND

0   500 Miles

0   500 KM

КАРТА МИРА

ARCTIC OCEAN

GREENLAND

Baffin Bay

ICELAND

Bering Sea

CANADA

ALEUTIAN ISLANDS

NORTH AMERICA

Hudson Bay

UNITED STATES OF AMERICA

ATLANTIC OCEAN

AZORES (Portugal)

MOROCCO

BERMUDA

CANARY ISLANDS (Spain)

WESTERN SAHARA

HAWAIIAN ISLANDS (US)

MEXICO

Gulf of Mexico

THE BAHAMAS

CUBA

DOMINICAN REPUBLIC

PUERTO RICO

SENEGAL

MAURITANIA

CAPE VERDE

JAMAICA

BELIZE

HAITI

GUINEA-BISSAU

GAMBIA

GUINEA

BURK FAS

PACIFIC OCEAN

GUATEMALA

HONDURAS

EL SALVADOR

NICARAGUA

SIERRA LEONE

COT D'IVO

COSTA RICA

VENEZUELA

GUYANA

LIBERIA

GHAN

PANAMA

SURINAME

FRENCH GUIANA

LINE ISLANDS

COLOMBIA

EQUATOR GUINEA

PHOENIX ISLANDS

Equator

GALÁPAGOS ISLANDS

ECUADOR

SOUTH AMERICA

KIRIBATI

AMERICAN SAMOA

MARQUESAS ISLANDS

PERU

BRAZIL

COOK ISLANDS

WESTERN SAMOA

FRENCH POLYNESIA

BOLIVIA

TONGA

TAHITI

SOCIETY ISLANDS

PARAGUAY

AUSTRAL ISLANDS

CHILE

ARGENTINA

URUGUAY

N

W   E

S

FALKLAND/MALVINAS ISLANDS

TIME ZONES
ЧАСОВЫЕ ПОЯСА

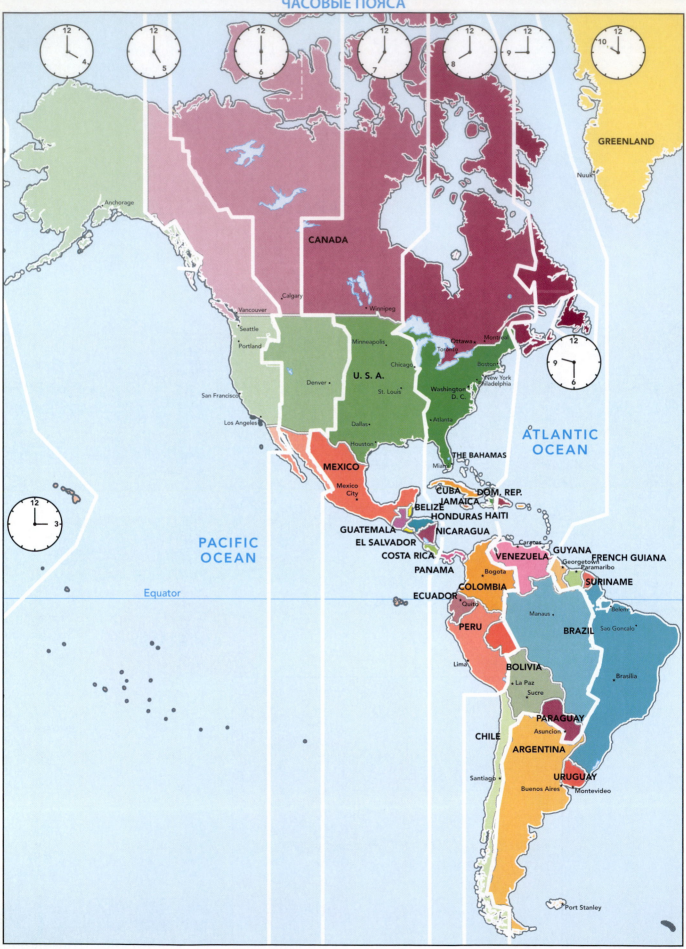

СТРАНЫ, НАЦИОНАЛЬНОСТИ И ЯЗЫКИ

Country	Nationality	Language		Country	Nationality	Language
Afghanistan	Afghan	Afghan		Italy	Italian	Italian
Argentina	Argentine	Spanish		Japan	Japanese	Japanese
Australia	Australian	English		Jordan	Jordanian	Arabic
Bolivia	Bolivian	Spanish		Korea	Korean	Korean
Brazil	Brazilian	Portuguese		Laos	Laotian	Laotian
Bulgaria	Bulgarian	Bulgarian		Latvia	Latvian	Latvian
Cambodia	Cambodian	Cambodian		Lebanon	Lebanese	Arabic
Canada	Canadian	English/French		Lithuania	Lithuanian	Lithuanian
Chile	Chilean	Spanish		Malaysia	Malaysian	Malay
China	Chinese	Chinese		Mexico	Mexican	Spanish
Colombia	Colombian	Spanish		New Zealand	New Zealander	English
Costa Rica	Costa Rican	Spanish		Nicaragua	Nicaraguan	Spanish
Cuba	Cuban	Spanish		Norway	Norwegian	Norwegian
(The) Czech Republic	Czech	Czech		Pakistan	Pakistani	Urdu
Denmark	Danish	Danish		Panama	Panamanian	Spanish
(The) Dominican Republic	Dominican	Spanish		Peru	Peruvian	Spanish
Ecuador	Ecuadorian	Spanish		(The) Philippines	Filipino	Tagalog
Egypt	Egyptian	Arabic		Poland	Polish	Polish
El Salvador	Salvadorean	Spanish		Portugal	Portuguese	Portuguese
England	English	English		Puerto Rico	Puerto Rican	Spanish
Estonia	Estonian	Estonian		Romania	Romanian	Romanian
Ethiopia	Ethiopian	Amharic		Russia	Russian	Russian
Finland	Finnish	Finnish		Saudi Arabia	Saudi	Arabic
France	French	French		Slovakia	Slovak	Slovak
Germany	German	German		Spain	Spanish	Spanish
Greece	Greek	Greek		Sweden	Swedish	Swedish
Guatemala	Guatemalan	Spanish		Switzerland	Swiss	German/French/Italian
Haiti	Haitian	Haitian Kreyol		Taiwan	Taiwanese	Chinese
Honduras	Honduran	Spanish		Thailand	Thai	Thai
Hungary	Hungarian	Hungarian		Turkey	Turkish	Turkish
India	Indian	Hindi		Ukraine	Ukrainian	Ukrainian
Indonesia	Indonesian	Indonesian		(The) United States	American	English
Israel	Israeli	Hebrew		Venezuela	Venezuelan	Spanish
				Vietnam	Vietnamese	Vietnamese

A. Where are you from?
B. I'm from **Mexico**.

A. What's your nationality?
B. I'm **Mexican**.

A. What language do you speak?
B. I speak **Spanish**.

Tell about yourself: Where are you from? What's your nationality? What languages do you speak?

Now interview and tell about a friend.

СПИСКИ ГЛАГОЛОВ

Правильные Глаголы

Правильные глаголы имеют четыре разных написания прошедшего времени и причастия прошедшего времени.

1 Добавьте **–ed** на конец глагола. Например:

act → act**ed**

act	cook	grill	pass	simmer
add	correct	guard	peel	sort
answer	cough	hand (in)	plant	spell
appear	cover	help	play	sprain
ask	crash	insert	polish	steam
assist	cross (out)	invent	pour	stow
attack	deliver	iron	print	stretch
attend	deposit	kick	reach	surf
bank	design	land	record	swallow
board	discuss	leak	register	talk
boil	dress	learn	relax	turn
box	drill	lengthen	repair	twist
brainstorm	dust	lift	repeat	unload
broil	edit	listen	request	vacuum
brush	end	load	respond	vomit
burn	enter	look	rest	walk
burp	establish	lower	return	wash
carpool	explain	mark	roast	watch
cash	faint	match	rock	wax
check	fasten	mix	saute	weed
clean	fix	mow	scratch	whiten
clear	floss	obey	seat	work
collect	fold	open	select	
comb	follow	paint	shorten	
construct	form	park	sign	

2 Добавьте **–d** на конец глагола который заканчивается на **–e**. Например:

assemble → assemble**d**

assemble	declare	grate	pronounce	shave
bake	describe	hire	prune	slice
balance	dislocate	manage	raise	sneeze
barbecue	dive	measure	rake	state
bathe	dribble	microwave	recite	style
bounce	enforce	move	recycle	supervise
browse	erase	nurse	remove	translate
bruise	examine	operate	revise	type
bubble	exchange	organize	rinse	underline
change	exercise	overdose	save	unscramble
circle	experience	practice	scrape	use
close	file	prepare	serve	vote
combine	gargle	produce	share	wheeze

3 Удвойте последнюю согласную и добавьте **–ed** на конец глагола. Например:

chop → chop**ped**

chop	mop	skip	transfer
hop	plan	stir	trim
knit	occur	stop	

4 Уберите –y и добавьте **–ied** на конец глагола. Например:

apply → appl**ied**

apply	dry	fry	study
copy	empty	stir-fry	try

Неправильные Глаголы

Нижеперечисленные глаголы имеют прошедшее время и/или причастия прошедшего времени которые не подчиняются правилам.

be	was/were	been		know	knew	known
beat	beat	beaten		leave	left	left
become	became	become		let	let	let
bend	bent	bent		make	made	made
begin	began	begun		meet	met	met
bleed	bled	bled		pay	paid	paid
break	broke	broken		put	put	put
bring	brought	brought		read	read	read
build	built	built		rewrite	rewrote	rewritten
buy	bought	bought		run	ran	run
catch	caught	caught		ring	rang	rung
choose	chose	chosen		say	said	said
come	came	come		see	saw	seen
cut	cut	cut		sell	sold	sold
do	did	done		set	set	set
draw	drew	drawn		shoot	shot	shot
drink	drank	drunk		sing	sang	sung
drive	drove	driven		sit	sat	sat
eat	ate	eaten		sleep	slept	slept
fall	fell	fallen		speak	spoke	spoken
feed	fed	fed		stand	stood	stood
fly	flew	flown		sweep	swept	swept
get	got	gotten		swim	swam	swum
give	gave	given		swing	swung	swung
go	went	gone		take	took	taken
grow	grew	grown		teach	taught	taught
hang	hung	hung		throw	threw	thrown
have	had	had		understand	understood	understood
hit	hit	hit		withdraw	withdrew	withdrawn
hold	held	held		write	wrote	written
hurt	hurt	hurt				

Цифры написанные выделенным шрифтом указывают на какой странице находится слово. Цифры написанные обычным шрифтом указывают на местонахождение слова в иллюстрации и в списке слов. Например "адрес **1**-5" указывает что слово *адрес* находится на странице 1 и является предметом под номером пять.

The bold number indicates the page(s) on which the word appears. The number that follows indicates the word's location in the illustration and in the word list on the page. For example, "address **1**-5" indicates that the word *address* is on page 1 and is item number 5.